To George Hofman
with my best regards

Walter Hoving

THE DISTRIBUTION REVOLUTION

The Distribution Revolution

by

Walter Hoving

IVES WASHBURN, INC.

New York

CONTENTS

FOREWORD

Ever since the advent of the industrial revolution more than one hundred years ago the world has been grappling with the problems of absorbing the goods that have been turned out in ever-increasing quantities by our constantly improving and rapidly growing production machines.

This revolution literally changed the world. It changed it not only from an economic point of view, but sociologically, physiologically, psychologically, and even spiritually.

It brought about the final demise of the feudal system

which could no longer exist under the emerging capitalist order, itself a child of the industrial revolution. And it was the direct cause of the socialist and Marxist philosophy that has finally split the world into two armed and antagonistic camps.

It has also been the direct cause of the cyclically recurring booms and busts that have done almost as much damage to humanity in the last one hundred years as the great epidemics and pestilences of the Middle Ages did in their time.

Are there any solutions to these world-wide economic problems?

I believe there are. I believe the solutions will be found in what we do *after* we produce our products; in short, the solutions will be found largely in the field of distribution rather than in the field of production.

Last year I put my thoughts into a paper that I read at one of the Tobé lectures at the Harvard Graduate School of Business Administration. I called it "The Distribution Revolution." I received so many requests for copies of this lecture that I decided to expand it into a small book, and here it is.

In it I have attempted to state the principles involved in the process of distribution in simple, uncomplicated language so that the man in the street, who in the final analysis must apply them, can easily understand them.

W.H.

New York
July, 1960

THE DISTRIBUTION REVOLUTION

THE DISTRIBUTION REVOLUTION

1

WHAT IS MASS DISTRIBUTION?

There is a great deal of talk these days about mass production. Everyone seems interested in the subject. You hear statistics about steel production, about electric power production in the most unexpected places. And factories for producing all sorts of things are being built everywhere.

The benefits of mass production have been so widely advertised that all over the world, especially in the Soviet Union, in Africa, in South and Central America, in Red China and India, people are scrambling to get into mass production of every conceivable product.

Some people even seem to think that mass production can cure all the world's economic and social ills. You might almost say that it has become a world mania. Mass production has become our god, our cure-all, our economic savior.

When Nikita Khrushchev visited the United States last year, he talked constantly about Russia's program of mass production. He claimed that eventually Russia was going to outproduce the United States. The goal of the Soviets, according to Mr. Khrushchev, was first to catch up with the United States and then to outstrip us. His five-year plans and seven-year plans are all gaited to this end, and the Russian people are constantly being urged to bend every effort to achieve these goals.

Incentive systems and stretch-out systems are being instituted in Russian factories that no American union or respectable workingman would tolerate. Stakhanovites are given Soviet decorations if they can outdo their fellow workers, and special privileges of all sorts are offered if they can exceed their norms and produce more than their quotas.

But, nowhere in his talks did Khrushchev say anything about distribution. As a matter of fact he didn't seem to be aware of this side of the economic picture at all. He seemed to think production is the alpha and omega of the economic system.

The answer is, of course, that he seems to know little about mass distribution. He has no conception of the role it plays in the American production-distribution system. Nor does he understand that mass production cannot be separated from mass distribution, that neither can function without the other.

Visitors who have come back from Red China say they are busy building factories. And these are good factories, too, planned and supervised by European and Soviet engineers. Some of them are better than many of ours, because they are new and have newer machinery.

But these visitors also tell us that many of the factories in Red China don't seem to be functioning. In some of them hardly a wheel is turning. The factory hands either sit around listening to political lectures or keep busy making handmade things, some for their own use. The wheels of the factories just stand still. Why?

Because Red China has no system of distribution and consequently there are no developed markets for the products of these factories. The Red Chinese have no conception of how to build a system of distribution or the intricacies of its operation. Nor do they understand the necessary economic climate for the distribution process.

One should not minimize the difficulties or the intricacies of the production process because it takes great skill and organization to mass-produce. It is not the purpose of this book, however, to dwell on the problems of production, because much has been written and said about them during recent years.

But it seems to me that there is so little understanding of the theories and practices of distribution and its role in the world economy that it is about time people's attention began to be focused on it.

My objective is to delve more deeply into the fundamental principles of distribution because unless the world makes some real progress in this area it will end up in a mass production jam.

Now the industrial revolution began a little more than a hundred years ago with the introduction of steam power and the use of machinery in the production of goods. This was a tremendous step in the history of civilization because it introduced the new principle that man can successfully produce more than he can individually consume if he multiplies his efforts by using a machine.

Since then electric power has to a great extent replaced steam power, and important inventions in machinery, in metal alloys, and in the knowledge of engineering have caused tremendous strides to be made. Atomic power is just peeking over the horizon. When it becomes practical its development will help to manufacture power that is more readily available and cheaper than ever before.

Skillful techniques that tend toward greater automation are also making it possible for a worker to produce more than ever before. He simply pushes buttons and thereby tends to more machinery than his ancestors could take care of when steam power became available in the first half of the nineteenth century.

There is no question that more and more goods will be produced at less and less cost as the years go on. Mankind will be able to enjoy the ever-increasing leisure automation is creating and will continue to create in the future.

But while this revolution in production has been

taking place, another lesser noticed revolution has been going on, too. It came a little later and evolved more slowly. It evolved more slowly because it was more intricate and created even greater problems than mass production. This was the revolution in distribution.

Mass production had created severe economic cycles that had not existed in the world before. Depressions for centuries had been caused almost entirely by droughts and famines or by war. But mass production introduced a new factor. From time to time it produced more goods than the public seemed able to consume. Consequently production would grind to a halt and many people were thrown out of work. Why did this happen periodically?

The fact was that we did not have a fully developed system of mass distribution. Nor did we understand very clearly the principles needed to create it. Because of this failure to distribute properly the goods our machines turned out, many people began to feel there was something basically wrong with the world. Criticism began to be heard about the capitalistic system.

Karl Marx picked up the cudgels, claiming the capitalistic system was at fault because goods could not be distributed after they were produced. He said the profit motive was at fault; if we could only ditch this factor everything would be all right. He put forth the idea that every man should produce according to his ability, and implied that we should distribute to every man according to his need.

At the time Marx blasted the capitalistic sytem, there was very little understanding in any quarter about the interrelationships of production and distribution, and the periodic depressions caused by the faulty and under-developed distribution system brought much human misery. People who had been taken off the farms and given jobs in fast-growing factory towns because of the burgeoning industrial activity would be discharged and left to walk the streets whenever overproduction developed a glut in the market.

Many followers of Marx felt that the problem of distribution could not be solved except by introducing an entirely new social order. Today many socialists of various hues advocate changing the socioeconomic system as the solution of the problem. They vaguely recognize that there can be no sustained mass production without mass distribution. But they think it necessary to change the system if mass distribution is to work. They decry the economic ups and downs, the booms and busts, claiming they are all the fault of the capitalistic system. They say we must take the means of production from private hands and put them into the hands of the government in order to make everything work properly.

Now this has been tried in Russia for more than forty years. However, there is as yet no indication that capital owned and managed by a government works any better than it does in private hands. As a matter of fact the evidence points to the opposite conclusion.

It is interesting to note in this connection that the word "capitalism" is a poor description of the private-property system because a socialistic or communistic system is also capitalism. The chief difference lies in the fact that under capitalism capital is privately managed and owned, whereas in the communistic and socialistic systems capital is in the hands of the government, which is responsible for its utilization and management. There is actually no possibility in the twentieth century of operating without capital, whether it be privately or publicly owned.

We in America have demonstrated better than any other country that when you understand the principles of mass distribution the social system not only does not need to be changed, but mass distribution works infinitely better if you don't change it. There is no question in my mind that the American capitalistic system is the best possible socioeconomic system (in spite of its human defects), and the only one that can make the mass-production-distribution system work for the benefit of all.

Apparently the world has not yet learned this lesson. Many so-called neutral countries such as India, and certain of the countries now gaining independence in Africa, feel that they've got to try the socialistic way of achieving general well-being for their people. The facts indicate, however, that although governments can often build factories as well as private industry and sometimes even operate them fairly well, no government in the history of the world has yet been able to organize an efficient system of distribution. Only personal initiative functioning under the system of private enterprise has ever been able to do this.

This is because such a system requires people to run it who have grown up under a regime that teaches personal responsibility and self-discipline. These qualities can be acquired only in an atmosphere of freedom.

The exact opposite of such a climate is the Soviet system, which initiates all discipline from above. People obey the laws because they fear the bureaucracy and its secret police, rather than because they have accepted a moral code that has been ingrained during their adolescent years.

This lack of self-discipline under communism has been lately demonstrated in Poland, where the Soviet kind of government discipline has completely demoralized large sections of the population. It shows itself in excessive drunkenness and a tremendous increase in theft, both of which have been fairly common in Russia as well.

But distribution is an intricate process with many interrelated factors in every one of which resourcefulness, responsibility, and personal competence are of the essence. None of these things can operate effectively under bureaucratic control. They can be used only by people who have grown up in freedom and have learned to take care of themselves, to discipline themselves, to guide themselves.

These are the reasons why mass distribution will never really succeed under the communistic or socialistic type of government. This political climate simply does not breed the kind of human beings that can perform on their own.

What most of the world needs to learn from an economic point of view is a better understanding of the principles of mass distribution and how to put them into practice. Unless this great revolution in distribution becomes world wide, the determined drive for mass production will continue to cause periodic economic depressions as it has in the past.

Therefore it is important to examine the principles of distribution. What are some of them? How do they work? In the following chapters I will try to cover thirteen of the basic principles of distribution without which mass production will not work.

CHAPTER

2

THE PRINCIPLE
OF SELF-CONSUMPTION

I call the first principle *self-consumption*. This is based on the discovery, an American discovery incidentally, that the man who makes the product must be one of its major consumers. In other words, the factory hand who is producing, let us say an automobile, must be able to buy one for his own use. If the automobile is sold only to the people sitting up in the front office, or to the people in the upper-income brackets, there can, of course, be no mass production.

This idea is contrary to all past history. Going back

five thousand years one finds that artisans generally made things for other people to consume. The artisan was hardly ever paid enough money to buy the product himself.

In the Middle Ages the artisans formed guilds in order to monopolize their particular crafts. In England they received charters from the Crown, which gave them the right to do business in certain areas.

Much of the work of these guilds, however, was done by apprentices who received no pay. As a matter of fact, they often had to pay for the privelege of working in the guilds, very much as students now pay for school or college. The master craftsmen were the only individuals who made enough money to live in reasonable comfort. Consequently, it was rather unusual when other members of the guild made enough money to consume the products they made.

With the introduction of the industrial system in the middle of the nineteenth century, people were lured off the big estates and brought into the cities to work in factories. They were paid such low wages they could barely buy necessities and sometimes not even those. Child labor was freely used and its output was sold entirely to the well-to-do. This system is fairly common even today in most parts of the world with the exception of America and certain parts of Europe. In most factories the factory hands don't make enough money to consume the products they manufacture.

This is because too many countries in the world believe their well-being depends upon their export business. To a considerable degree this is true. Thus they resist paying higher wages so they can compete in the world's markets, especially in the American market.

Today we are seeing a great influx of goods from Japan, Hong Kong, and other areas of the world, the prices of which are based on this cheap labor factor. The prevailing wage in Hong Kong today is from forty cents to a dollar a day for unskilled labor and from one dollar to three dollars a day for skilled labor.

Until these countries realize their domestic market is at least equal in value to their export markets and that their domestic market depends on paying their workers enough to enable them to become consumers of their own products, they will not have the prosperity they need to support their own people.

For several hundred years England was the great producer of fine silverware. Today there are very few silver factories in England producing good-quality silverware. They ruined their domestic market by putting an abnormally high purchase tax on silverware during and after the war in a foolish and misguided effort to increase their export market for silver. Now they have found out that without a good domestic market to sustain production, the export market alone is not enough, particularly in the quality fields.

The same thing was true in fine gold and diamond jewelry. England used to be a major producer of this merchandise, but an abnormally high purchase tax ruined the domestic market, and today England is not even a factor in this industry.

However, England is still producing fine worsted and woolen materials because she has always had a good domestic market for these things. As a result manufacturers can get economic runs on this merchandise in order to produce at reasonable prices. This made it possible to compete with the rest of the world on a very favorable basis.

The fact is that those countries that depend upon the export market almost exclusively are simply fooling themselves in the long run. Without the principle of self-consumption that enables their workmen to earn enough to be important consumers of their products no sustained prosperity within any country is possible.

We hear a great deal of talk about America pricing herself out of the foreign market because of our high wages. Undoubtedly there is some danger of this happening in certain areas. But in many lines of merchandise, where we have a broad consumption because of the excellent wages our factory workers are paid, there is little chance we can be outpriced. For example, in the coal industry we can pay our miners three to four times as much as some of the miners get in Europe; yet we can produce and land coal in Europe for less money than they can produce coal at their own pitheads. By paying our miners more and investing in better machinery and better equipment, we can mine more efficiently than many other countries.

The same is true in the automobile business. A domestic market that will consume from five to six million cars a year gives us an enormous advantage in mass production and enables us to produce efficiently enough automobiles to sell all over the world. If the countries that have placed embargoes and restrictions on our products to prevent us from capturing their markets would remove them, we would sell many more. And everyone knows that one reason for this efficient production is the high wage that the automobile industry pays the worker.

England has just lifted her embargo on American ready-to-wear. This gives us access to the British market with our clothing products, which we produce so efficiently. Indications are that we will now do a very satisfactory export business with the British Isles in this field.

So far the facts do not seem to indicate that we are pricing ourselves out of the export market. In the twelve months ended September, 1959, our exports were $9,200,000,000 and our imports were $4,800,000,000. So we had an excess of exports of $4,400,000,000 in that twelve-month period. This is no cause for panic.

In every major classification we import some goods while our factories make substantial exports. Here are some figures:

Machine Tools	Exports	$156,000,000
	Imports	30,000,000
	Net Exports	$126,000,000
Agriculture Equipment	Exports	$141,000,000
	Imports	112,000,000
	Net Exports	$ 29,000,000
Engines and Parts	Exports	$232,000,000
	Imports	5,000,000
	Net Exports	$227,000,000
Consumer Goods (Excluding Foods and Textiles)	Exports	$890,000,000
	Imports	876,000,000
	Net Exports	$ 14,000,000

THE PRINCIPLE OF SELF-CONSUMPTION

Now let us take a classification in which we have had some stiff foreign competition—textiles. Although we import more textiles than we export, our exports are still fairly substantial.

Textiles		
	Imports	$591,000,000
	Exports	434,000,000
	Net Imports	$157,000,000

Of course what these foreign manufacturers are doing is to take advantage of our fully developed distribution machinery. If the American domestic market did not exist, the production of the rest of the world would be very much smaller. Perhaps Congress will eventually have to regulate this in one way or another for the protection of American labor. It is only logical for us to protect ourselves from manufacturers who do little to develop their own domestic markets, but who insist on using ours to their own advantage.

A more recent trend is a movement on the part of our own manufacturers to move plants abroad and then bring the products back and sell them in the American market. This will continue so long as a serious wage differential exists, which in turn depends on the lack of understanding abroad of the principles that have created the distribution revolution.

Thirty-five years ago, when I first started in the retail business, the average sales clerk was paid approximately $18.00 to $20.00 a week. Today the average sales clerk is paid from $50.00 to $70.00 per week and has become an important consumer of this country's products.

It is interesting to note that last year 19 per cent of

the total pay roll of Bonwit Teller, a large New York specialty store, was spent right in the store. In other words, the salespeople and all the other employees, executive and non-executive, spent almost 20 per cent of their earnings buying things for themselves and their families from Bonwit Teller.

I remember years ago visiting on Prince's Bay, Staten Island, and seeing workmen going to work at the S.S. White Company factory on the water front on their bicycles. Hundreds and hundreds of bicycles arrived in the morning and left in the evening. In those days hardly anyone owned an automobile. Today almost all these workmen are paid enough so that they can afford to have a car, which makes it possible to place factories in the open country as long as they are accessible to main roads.

A drive through the countryside on any weekday will take one past the cars parked in the parking lots of one-story modern factories. These cars, of course, are owned by the workmen themselves. If they weren't, it would not be possible to locate these factories out in the country in the open fields. Otherwise the factories would be huddled in cities and small towns.

The fact is that if more factories are built in the so-called backward countries and if more goods are produced with sweat-shop labor, the world will get into more of a jam economically. This will raise a hue and cry against the United States. These countries will complain that it is all our fault because we won't let them dump their products on our market.

All these countries feel they have a vested right to sell a large share of their products in this country. It doesn't seem to have occurred to them that their primary responsibility is to cultivate their domestic markets. To accomplish this they must first pay their workers a better-than-living wage so that they can become consumers of these products.

This is one of the simple truths that is so simple it is too much for most people to grasp. The average factory owner abroad, whether he be a private individual or the government, seems to feel that the less he pays his workers the better chance he has to sell his product. If this had been the American philosophy during the last fifty years we would certainly not be where we are today. We could never have developed such a prosperous country on that basis. Our theory of self-consumption, as a matter of fact, is quite the opposite, and it is one of the fundamental principles upon which our economy has been built.

How does this principle of self-consumption operate in our economy?

In the year 1940 we produced 3,717,000 passenger cars and in 1959 we produced approximately 5,500,000 cars.

Today there are 213,000,000 radio and television sets in use in the United States. This includes 106,000,000 in homes, 14,000,000 in business places or institutions, 40,000,000 automobile radios, and 52,000,000 television sets. In all the rest of the world there are only 171,900,000. The United States has much more than half of all the sets in use today.

Electric-power production, too, has gone up from 127,000,000,000 kilowatt hours in 1939 to 707,000,000,-000 kilowatt hours in 1959.

Let's take a look at motor fuel. In 1945 we consumed 696,000,000 barrels of petroleum. In 1958 we consumed 1,422,000,000 barrels. This gives a pretty fair idea of the increase in consumption in the United States and how it has been affected by the increased prosperity of the wage earner.

3

A CONSTANTLY INCREASING INCOME

The second principle on which mass distribution rests is *a constantly increasing income*. This logically follows the principle of self-consumption described in the preceding chapter. This principle rests on the premise that unless a worker is paid a wage that rises steadily, there can be no steady rise in the distribution pattern. This, of course, must evolve gradually and slowly. During the last seventy-five years it has produced our American high standard of living.

This has not been achieved simply by decreeing it.

It has been a struggle and sometimes a rather painful one. Labor has of course been constantly striving for higher wages. But management, too, in America has taken a much more enlightened attitude about this matter.

There have been labor unions for many more years in Europe than in America, but wages there have not been improved anything like as much as they have in America. The main reason for this is that a very large part of management in this country has had a very constructive attitude toward wages. Not all, by any means, but a goodly portion of management has always felt that a gradually rising wage scale would be a benefit to the country at large. It has been understood much more clearly here than in other parts of the world that mass distribution is possible only if the workingman is able to be one of the country's best customers.

It was a sensation all over the world when Henry Ford announced his $5.00-a-day minimum wage. Some people even in this country felt that it would ruin America if such a high wage became a general thing. But as the years rolled on, most industrialists followed Mr. Ford's lead and raised wages first to $5.00 and then to much higher levels. Of course, $5.00 a day now seems ridiculous in the United States. But there are many parts of the world where even $5.00 a week is considered a high wage.

Hourly wages here in the last fifteen years have gone up from $1.02 to $2.23 and the weekly average earnings have gone from $44.00 per week to $90.00 per week in the same period. Consider what this has done to increase distribution in this country.

In this connection it is interesting to note how the national income has been affected by the constantly rising wage rates. In the last thirty years the percentage of wages of the total personal income in the United States has gone up from 59 per cent in 1929 to 70 per cent in 1959. In the same period the percentage of dividend income to the whole has gone down from 6.8 per cent in 1929 to 3.5 per cent last year. This economic pattern is very significant. It shows we have a distribution economy rather than a production economy in America today.

Further proof of this changing economic pattern is shown by the significant shift in employment in the United States.

In the production field there has been a constant shift from the farms to industry. Whereas the number of people employed in agriculture has dropped 45 per cent in the last thirty years, nonagricultural employment has gone up 55 per cent.

But the increase in employment in the field of distribution has been even more significant, showing that the revolution in distribution has had a tremendous impact on the American economy. The figures show a rise of 74 per cent in wholesale and retail employment and an even greater rise of more than 100 per cent in the service trades in the last thirty years.

As a matter of fact ever since 1953 we have had more people employed in the distribution and service fields than in the production industries. Consequently the year 1953 marks one of the most significant events in the economic history of the world, because this was the first time in any country that employment in distribution exceeded employment in production, thus heralding the advent of the distribution age.

Of course a rising wage rate would not of itself do the job. In fact, it would be inflationary. It must always be coupled with *A slightly more rapid increase in the production per worker than in the wages of that worker.* This is the second part of this great principle that helped create the revolution in distribution in America.

Not long ago there was a big hassle in the steel industry. The union leaders felt that wages should be raised without regard to the productivity per worker. Management felt, of course, that if they raised wages and then had to raise prices it would be simply inflationary. In my opinion, there is no question that they were right.

Many union leaders have not yet learned this principle. But unless there is a more rapid increase in the production per worker than in his wage, you cannot have a real increase in his income. And only such a real increase improves the buying power of the public.

Such an increase in the per-capita income cannot be developed overnight. It will take time to develop it in South America, Africa, or in Asia. Also, in my opinion, it can evolve only if the economic philosophy permits it to do so.

A friend of mine who had returned from Russia told me that he visited a large shoe factory in Moscow. He reported that the processes were all very slow and there was too much wasted labor. He said the quality of the shoes was simply appalling. If they were offered for sale in the United States he doubted whether they could be sold for $2.00 a pair.

The price in Moscow, however, was about $25.00 a pair. It is amazing that there are any Russians who can afford to buy shoes at such high prices. Twenty-five dollars for shoes is a pretty high price even in the United States, where real wages are much higher than they are in Rusisa. But he said the total number of shoes turned out in Russia is so small they can sell them without any trouble.

This of course, does not create mass distribution or make more and better shoes for the public. But it clearly illustrates the economic philosophy of the Soviets. Theirs is a high-profit economy in the truest sense. They preach against profits, but they don't practice what they preach. In this case they produce shoddy merchandise at low wages. Then the government marks it up very high, and because of the scarcity of shoes, gets away with it. This, of course, won't build a rising level of prosperity. It is the age-old technique of sweating labor to make enough profit to feed the plutocrats and run the Soviet bureaucracy's projects. It explains how they get the money they need for their moon shots and sputniks.

This principle of a constantly increasing income based upon increasing production per worker seems to be very difficult for people to grasp. Many people in our own country not only do not seem to understand it, but they resist it. Self-seeking union leaders and economically ignorant people feel that if they can push up the wages in their particular industry, the workers in other industries can worry about themselves.

Such tactics, which are only too familiar to all of us, lead rather rapidly to economic dislocations, and adjustments known as recessions and depressions are necessary to iron them out. Depressions are a pretty painful way of straightening out these things, with their toll in human suffering.

We have learned that the dog-eat-dog philosophy which is still in vogue in so many parts of the world just doesn't pay. It is often practiced by ambitious labor leaders who try to gain status in their own locals, thus enabling them to become more important in their international unions. Their knowledge of the workings of the total economy is often so meager that it isn't surprising they have little understanding of what makes things tick. The way to avoid depressions is to have a clearer understanding of how distribution works.

However, there is no question that there is a greater understanding of such matters in the United States than in any other country in the world. If some of the underdeveloped countries could acquire some of our knowledge, the improvement in the well-being of their citizens would be very noticeable.

Too many people in the world seem to feel that the economic pie is of constant size and that their job is to fight for a bigger piece of it. This, by definition, would leave less for other people. We in America have learned, however, that the economic pie can be an ever-expanding one. And the bigger the slice one industry cuts, the more that industry contributes toward the growth of the total economy. This is one of the basic differences between the American and the European attitude toward the totality of economic possibilities. We have learned that the more each segment of the economy grows the better for everybody.

Far too many people outside the United States still seem to feel that the only way to get more business is to take it away from the other fellow, thus depriving him of what he already has. This philosophy is behind the narrow point of view that makes many people fight against increasing wages. They feel that wages must be kept as low as possible, instead of as high as possible, provided, of course—and this is the important point—that the production per worker increases faster than his wages. Belief in this simple truth is one of the main differences between the operation of the American economy and that of most of the rest of the world, and is one of the important reasons for the great strides mass distribution has made in this country.

4

THE ONE-PRICE PRINCIPLE

The third principle that exerts a very important influence on distribution is *the one-price principle*.

This may sound very simple to those of us who are used to it, but apparently others do not find it so.

My information is that it was invented by Tiffany & Co. more than a hundred years ago when Mr. Tiffany decided that it was not good business to bargain with the customer. So he decided to mark all his merchandise with a ticket, and that was the price. It could not be altered by anyone, even himself.

But this principle is by no means universally adhered

to. We find it practiced in England and in large cities around the world, but in other places you have to bargain with the storekeeper.

The main trouble with bargaining is that one has to spend a lot of time doing it. Not only must the customer spend a lot of time, but the storekeeper must also. Thus it takes so long to put through a transaction that distribution is slowed up to a tremendous degree. You cannot have mass distribution if the one-price principle is not followed, because the transaction time is just too long.

Hardly anyone goes into a store in Paris without trying to bargain for a better price. Some shops will not tolerate it, but many others on the Continent will cut the price if urged sufficiently.

One day a customer came to Tiffany and tried to get the store to lower a price. He said that a competitor had offered him a lower price than the original one, so why wouldn't Tiffany do the same? When the salesman said, "But they are a two-price house," he answered, "Don't tell me that. They're a six-price house."

Because the one-price system is so common in the United States, a customer hardly ever asks for a lower price. Thus, all transactions can be speeded up enormously because this one stumbling block has been eliminated.

But where many transactions entail haggling and bargaining it is easy to see how much time is wasted in the distribution process. It is said that in the Arab world the bazaar keepers just wouldn't be happy unless they could haggle. With them it's a form of amusement. It makes for conversation, it becomes a social occasion. The customer comes back many times and begins wherever he left off. But be it amusing or entertaining, it certainly doesn't make for rapid distribution. It only slows up the process of selling.

In India, I am told, one even haggles about the price of food, and it takes all morning for the housewife to buy the food she needs for the evening meal. Can you imagine haggling with the manager of an A. & P. store in the United States? What do you suppose would happen to the business of that store? I don't believe it could do a fraction of the business it now does. Not only does the one-price principle speed up the process of selling, but it also eliminates a great many unnecessary clerks. You simply put your package in the pushcart and wheel it over to the checkout desk. The transactions are added up, the money is paid, and out you go. Few people realize how important it is to have the prices plainly marked on all packages. What an enormous timesaver this is, not only for each customer, but for the personnel as well.

It may be perfectly all right if people have plenty of time and don't think it important to distribute quantities of merchandise, but the one-price system is essential if the objective is more work for more people.

I am not very optimistic, however, about the rapid adoption of the one-price system throughout the rest of the world. The age-old bargaining habit has been so ingrained for so many thousands of years that it will take a long time to eliminate it.

A related factor is our practice of selling food in packages. This is another American invention. We sell hardly any food in open bins with the sole exception of a few vegetables.

It will take time to develop this custom in other countries. Recently a supermarket was opened in Rome, and it tried to sell packaged goods. It didn't work. It was forced to close because the housewives in Rome claimed that packaging ruined the flavor of the food, and they refused to patronize the store.

In the Soviet Union, I am told, all foods are exposed. They lie around on dirty tables, covered with flies, and look pretty unappetizing. This is true in most of Asia, Africa, and South America. Not only is it unsanitary, but it is a major deterrent to mass distribution.

Packaging of merchandise in America has been developed to a science. Costly studies are made of consumer preferences and much thought is given to making attractive packages that will appeal to the customer. Pretesting of small segments of the market goes on constantly to discover which package has the greatest consumer acceptance, then millions of dollars are invested in packaging machinery and materials.

Meats in the United States are now being packed in cellophane. This is a rather recent development. I understand it has increased the meat business substantially. This is another timesaver, because the housewife doesn't even have to talk to the butcher. She just picks up the cellophane-wrapped meat, on which the price is plainly marked, and puts it in her cart.

The manager of a chain grocery store made a rather interesting point to me about this new development. He said, "You know, many housewives don't know one piece of meat from another. Consequently, they are embarrassed to ask the butcher any questions because they are not anxious to show their ignorance. But now, with all this meat wrapped in cellophane and plainly marked, they are no longer embarrassed to show how little they know. This helps them to buy much more rapidly than ever before."

Of course this system requires open deep-freeze bins where the meat can be displayed, but more and more grocery stores throughout the United States have installed them. This was one of the things that intrigued Khrushchev when he went into a grocery store during his visit here. He seemed amazed and asked many questions about it. This same refrigerated counter also caused a great deal of interest in the American exhibition in Moscow some time ago.

Most customers don't like to ask a price because if it is too high they feel embarrassed for the sales clerk to think they can't afford it. Consequently, customers like to look at the price tickets themselves. If the price is too high, they merely move on to something else without embarrassment.

Another advantage of the one-price system is that the salespeople themselves can complete the transaction. It is not necessary for the head of the store or one of his chief assistants to be called in. Thus, the fact that everyone knows that Tiffany never alters its prices makes it possible for people to come in and buy diamond rings or other high-priced articles without asking to see the head of the store. The transaction can be completed directly with the sales clerk on the floor.

THE ONE-PRICE PRINCIPLE

This cannot happen in any jewelry store in Europe, or many jewelry stores here, because the customer must see the head of the store and bargain for a price. No customer is going to spend thousands of dollars if he thinks that the price can be shaded, and obviously the only person who can quote the lowest price in the final analysis is the head of the store. This means, of course, that the boss has to take part in all the important transactions in the average jewelry store, and it is easy to see how much time that takes.

In Tiffany's, however, some transactions of more than $100,000 have been completed in less than twenty minutes because the customer knows that the quoted price will be the same from either the head of the house or the salesman.

It might be remarked that $100,000 transactions don't occur so frequently that the boss can't spend a little time on them and, of course, that is true. But in the range of transactions involving up to $25,000 at Tiffany or dresses at Bonwit Teller for say $1,000 or $2,000 it is a different story. Bonwit Teller sells many dresses above $1,000, and all these transactions are completed by the sales clerks. If the department heads or vice-presidents had to be called in to bargain with the customer it would create a mess and be impossible to do all the business that is done.

There is another important angle to the one-price principle, namely, that most customers feel it just isn't honest to charge some people more money than others for the same product. In other words, if you pay a certain price for something and find out later that your neighbor was given a lower price for the same merchandise because he bargained longer, you feel that the storekeeper has not been fair to you.

If anything slows up distribution and has done so all through the ages, it is the fact that too many buyers feel the storekeeper is not honest with them.

There are various ways, of course, in which a consumer can be cheated, but one of the ones he resents most is being overcharged. The storekeeper who does this is not going to do a very large business. Customers will avoid him because they're afraid of being overcharged. The fear of being overcharged is one of the great deterrents to moving quantities of merchandise rapidly in many parts of the world.

If the merchant marks his goods plainly and gets a reputation of sticking to his prices, then he is beginning to make a real contribution toward general prosperity in his country.

The merchant who has different prices for different people is doing more harm to his economy than he realizes. By not sticking to the one-price principle he fails to do his part toward increasing consumption. This will prevent mass distribution from functioning properly. It will lower the level of prosperity and make fewer jobs available.

Five-year plans in Russia, China, India, or any other place, beautiful factories and more engineers and technicians, are always possible, but unless at the same time you change the psychology of their storekeepers and get them to put in the one-price system, money and effort are wasted. Because all the new factories and all the technicians produced by efficient school systems are going to come a cropper on this ridiculously simple, seemingly unimportant little principle which says that the one-price system is an important key element in moving goods through the pipeline of distribution into the consumers' hands.

5

COMPULSORY COMPETITION

The fourth principle is that of *compulsory competition*.

It may sound paradoxical to talk about free enterprise in one breath and compulsory competition in another, but the American economic system contains both of these principles. Our laws say definitely that we have *got* to be competitive. It is not just permissive, in America it is actually *compulsory*.

This means that you can't get together with your competitor and agree to fix prices or restrict markets. This is against the law, but it is only against the law in America and in no other place in the world. These are the so-called antitrust laws which say it is unlawful to conspire to fix prices or in "concert of action" to agree on restricting markets.

Many businessmen are sometimes annoyed by these antitrust laws, and with just cause because in the past they have sometimes been administered in a punitive way. But by and large I think we are very fortunate to have them, even though we may get impatient with them every now and then. We are the only nation in the world that insists on competition by law and it's one of the great strengths of the American economy.

By this I don't mean fair-trade laws that permit a producer of a specialty to instruct his dealers to adhere to certain prices. That, of course, is an entirely different matter. I'm talking about the principle of getting together and agreeing with your *competitor* to fix prices. It is the prohibition of this practice that creates a very vigorous and healthy competition, and there is no question in my mind that this has been an important factor in building our great distributive system in America. It has forced everyone in business to take the hard road and be competitive, rather than the easy road, as in so many countries where business concerns get together and divide markets and agree on prices.

What effect does this have on mass distribution? It has several very important effects. In the first place, it makes for a hard-hitting, vigorous, and imaginative approach in all channels of distribution. Second, it means that people are competing for the attention of the consumer. Finally, it means that producers are constantly offering new and improved merchandise in order to get business.

Under the old-world system of agreeing on prices there is much less incentive for manufacturers to make improvements in their products, and very often competing manufacturers, after agreeing on the price, would simply sit tight and do nothing more.

In this country, however, new models are constantly put out, styling is improved, prices are lowered, in our bid for the consumer's dollar. It makes for a strong, dynamic economy that is constantly moving and in which new products and new materials are always being introduced.

Take, for example, the introduction of synthetic fibers. Rayons, Nylons, Dacrons, and a host of other fibers have been introduced, most of them originated in this country or at least seen their greatest development here. Our compulsory competitive approach has made for keen rivalry in these new fibers. And this competition has developed these new textiles enormously. In 1959 the consumption of man-made fibers was almost two million pounds. This is 20 per cent more than the year before. Man-made fibers represented about 30 per cent of all fibers consumed last year. About thirty years ago they were only 10 per cent of the total.

No manufacturer can just sit and be satisfied with something he has made because if he does, the next manufacturer will try to outdo him with something better or lower in price. People who have not been in business in America find it hard to understand how strong an incentive this is in developing distribution.

Europeans are often astonished at the tremendous

amount of competition in this country, but very few of them are in favor of their own governments' passing anti-trust laws similar to ours. It is much too comfortable to be able to call up your competitor and get him to agree on the price than it is to redesign your product or re-engineer your plant and come out with a product that will meet the one he has just improved.

Take the automobile business, for example. Every year all production is stopped for almost two months while hundreds of millions of dollars are spent in re-tooling and realigning production lines for the annual model change-over. Few people realize the enormous significance of this maneuver. Each automobile manu-facturer hopes to outdo the others with more interesting, more intriguing, and more alluring models in competi-tion for the consumer's dollar.

In Europe they hardly ever do this. They run pretty much the same models year after year, although lately they have begun to adopt certain phases of the American change-over system. They feel it is wasteful for us to spend so much money each year in tooling up for our new models.

However, one need only point to the 5,500,000 auto-mobiles that were manufactured in the United States in 1959 in comparison with the few that are made abroad to see what effect this hard-hitting competition has had on the American market. It is a ruthless and a strenuous game, the American competitive game, but it has cer-tainly been a key factor in building up the mass distri-bution of goods in this country. Of course there is also competition abroad, and very strenuous competition, too. But it isn't anything like as vigorous and hard-hitting as it is under our compulsory competitive system.

This concept of a compulsory free-enterprise system is a unique American development that exists in no other place in the world. An example of how it is enforced occurred in the spring of 1959 in Philadelphia. A Federal grand jury brought criminal antitrust charges against the biggest and most important electrical companies in the United States. These indictments were the result of a year-long investigation of the electrical industry by the Justice Department, and these cases involved annual sales of more than $200,000,000. The total business under inquiry by this grand jury was between $1,000,000,000 and $2,000,000,000.

Indictments alleged a conspiracy among executives of these companies to allocate among themselves the percentage of business each would get on specific products, 42 per cent for one company, 38 per cent another, etc.

The executives of these companies met dozens of times, said the Government, in cities all around the country, to arrange their prices and bids, and they used code names in communicating with each other. On some items the companies agreed to raise prices simultaneously. All these practices are illegal and strictly forbidden. The maximum penalty for a violation under the Sherman Antitrust Act is a fine of $50,000, and in the case of the individuals possibly a year in prison.

The seriousness of the case was indicated by the board chairman of the largest electric company involved. In an extraordinary statement he said he had learned from the grand jury's investigation for the first time that certain of his officials had violated the company's policy of strict compliance with the antitrust laws.

These officials' legal punishment "could be most severe," he said, but because the company had its own responsibility, he had demoted the offenders and removed them from positions of responsibility. Among the officials were a vice-president and four general managers.

This is a good example of the kind of thing that is forbidden by law in the United States, and an overwhelming number of companies adhere strictly to these laws. No such laws, however, exist in Europe, and European manufacturers are amazed that we can think this kind of thing is anybody's business but his own. However, we have made it illegal, and there is no question that this type of compulsory competition has done much to help this country grow.

CHAPTER

6

A FREE BUT COMPETITIVE PRESS

The fifth principle that undergirds the mass distribution in the United States is *a free but competitive press*. There is a great difference between a press that is simply free and one that is also competitive. There is a free press in most of the free world. Under the private-enterprise system anybody who has enough capital can buy or start a newspaper. He can say pretty much what he pleases and still be protected under the laws guaranteeing a free press.

The importance of a free press in mass distribution is very often overlooked. As a matter of fact, a free economy could not possibly function without a free press.

In those countries where the Government has interfered with the freedom of the press it has not been long before restrictions are put on the rest of the private-property system as well. Conversely, if the Government begins interfering with the free-enterprise system, it isn't long before restrictions are also put on freedom of the press. The two are inseparably intertwined.

However, you cannot have a free press unless it is supported by advertising, and this must come from business corporations that are functioning under the free-enterprise system. And of course the more prosperous a country, the more advertising, which, in turn, makes the press freer and independent of governmental influences.

Many people abroad seem to feel that large corporations must have a great deal of influence over newspapers and magazines in this country because of the amount of money they spend advertising in them. This is an entirely erroneous idea. In my own experience no advertiser has had the slightest influence on the press, nor have I heard of any instances of it. The press in this country is very alert to any such influence and quick to resent it. No store in New York, even though it spent several millions of dollars in the New York newspapers each year, ever had the slightest influence on the editorial opinion of any newspaper, nor on any of the news that appears therein.

This, of course, is a very healthy situation, but to some foreigners a very paradoxical one. The Russians just don't believe it. They can't see how a press that is supported to such a large degree by its advertising revenue can help but be entirely controlled by the large corporations. It is true, nevertheless. Our press is free because it is supported by many thousands of advertisers. It needs no subsidy from the Government of any kind and therefore it has the means to combat any interference by governmental agencies or administrative bureaus.

This advertising support has been the chief factor in the success of so many newspapers and magazines, radio and television stations in this country. We have by far more newspaper and magazine circulation per capita than any other country in the world. This, in turn, furnishes the media necessary for mass advertising without which mass distribution, of course, cannot exist. We have our free press to thank for helping to move billions of dollars' worth of goods and services from the producer to the consumer every year.

But America also has a more competitive press than any other country in the world. Our laws require that the press must also be competitive. Newspapers are not allowed to agree on rates with their colleagues any more than manufacturers of merchandise or commodities are allowed to fix prices on their products.

One of the important London newspapers has a circulation of 250,000 a day. The *New York Times* has 675,000. However, you can buy a page in the *New York Times* for about a third of what you have to pay the London paper. Thus, the *New York Times* has almost three times the circulation but sells a page of advertising for a third of the London paper's price.

This is because some newspapers in Europe get together and say "Let's fix the rates," and then do so as high as they please, so high, in fact, that very few stores can afford to advertise in them frequently. That's why few department-store or other store advertisements appear in London papers. Most of the ads are concerned with nationally advertised products of various kinds.

When I talked with the head of one of London's big stores and asked him about this matter, he said, "Well, you know we can't afford to advertise very frequently in the newspapers. It's too expensive." The interesting thing is that the London paper mentioned above has even more advertising than our American papers. One entire page is devoted to personal ads for which satisfactory rates are charged. The last part of the paper contains statements by company chairmen or managing directors reporting upon the affairs of their corporations. Every line is paid advertising.

Now in almost all American papers such reports by company chairmen are printed for nothing. American papers are perfectly willing to give publicity to such statements in order to encourage business generally. Foreign papers do not; they charge for these things even though they don't put the word "advertisement" at the top, as is customary here, so that the reader cannot tell that this has been paid for.

Of course this kind of advertising may move stocks and bonds, but it certainly doesn't move merchandise, because the rates are so high that the stores cannot afford to buy very much space. The same thing is true in the papers in France and in many other European countries. They get together and fix the rates and keep them so high that the stores can't afford to advertise.

The papers abroad also get together and lobby vigorously against any competitive media such as commercial television or radio. Only in the last year or so has England licensed a station televising programs that also carries advertising. Up to that time there was only one channel in England and that was the B.B.C. The papers fought commercial television for years, carrying the torch on a high cultural level to convince people of the tawdriness of paid advertising over television. Actually, there are very few radio or television stations on the continent of Europe that are not operated by the government. We may be unhappy at times with the plethora of commercial advertising on our television programs. Sometimes we overdo this very seriously. Not only do the spot announcements often come too frequently, but they are also too long and too boring. But there isn't the slightest question that this advertising helps to move merchandise and move large quantities of it.

All of this adds up to the vital fact that there are not enough advertising media in the European markets to sell large quantities of merchandise to their own people. Here again their primary interest in the export market is an important influence. It is part and parcel of the philosophy that makes them neglect their own markets and emphasize their export trade.

When the rates for newspaper advertising and for magazine advertising are so high as to be almost prohibitive, and advertising through television and the radio is almost nonexistent, there is a very restricted market for goods.

There have also been instances of taxing advertising in European countries to discourage selling merchandise in domestic markets because the official government policy was to drive everything possible into the export field.

Billboards have always been more important in the European market than in America simply because of the difficulty of finding other channels of advertising. Everyone who has driven through Italy remembers how annoying it is to see billboard after billboard so thick along all the roads that it is almost impossible to see the scenery. All these billboards, incidentally, are owned and operated by the government and that is one more reason why the government is not anxious to let television enter the picture as a competitor of commercial advertising.

In Asia and Africa the situation is even more restricted I am told. Newspapers are not as plentiful as they are in Europe or in America and magazine circulation is very small indeed.

Thus, one can see how important a competitive press is in furnishing media for the spending of hundreds and hundreds of millions of dollars in moving merchandise through the distribution system.

CHAPTER

7

CONSUMER CONDITIONING

The sixth principle is called *consumer conditioning*. By this I mean the use of all the available avenues to condition, to educate, to inspire, and to interest the consumer to buy merchandise.

First of all, the most important way to condition consumers is through advertising.

Advertising in the United States, as we all know, is very highly developed. The most expert and the most professional talent is available to almost anyone in the distributive field through our talented and skilled advertising agencies. This is another American invention.

CONSUMER CONDITIONING

There were no advertising agencies until they were started in the United States, and there are no advertising agencies anywhere else that even begin to approach the skill and knowledge of almost any advertising agency in this country.

In addition, every department store, except perhaps the smallest, has its own advertising department, many of which are highly skilled and knowledgeable. These departments naturally become very familiar with the most effective methods for moving the merchandise of that particular store.

The amount of money spent on advertising in the United States staggers the imagination. I have never seen a figure that represents all of it, but it is certainly not less than $11,000,000,000 per year. There are a number of corporations that spend many millions of dollars in advertising each year. There is nothing comparable to these figures in the rest of the world.

It can be said without fear of contradiction that advertising is one of the strongest forces creating prosperity in the United States by conditioning the consumer to want the merchandise he consumes each year, thus causing an even flow of goods through the distribution channels. In this way we have built the enormous and unique prosperity which this country has achieved.

On the other hand, advertising in the rest of the world is far, far behind. As a matter of fact, many foreign businessmen have little faith in it. A Russian businessman revealed while visiting this country that they are not permitted any illustrations when they advertise in the Soviet newspapers. This is considered wasteful in the Soviet Union. There they are merely permitted to list their products in very small print. Such tactics will never help to build mass distribution or make for mass prosperity.

Someone in France told me last spring that he thought the reason France has the highest alcoholic consumption in the world was because the people are not conditioned through advertising to buy merchandise. Consequently, they are apt to get themselves a bottle of wine and a loaf of bread, and sometimes drink a little more than is good for them.

A bottle of wine may have its virtues, but it doesn't help create more wealth for more people. Plenty of liquor is drunk, of course, in America. But we don't consume anything like the amount of alcohol per capita that many countries in Europe do. Most of our people are too busy buying and paying for merchandise they have been preconditioned by advertising to want. This, of course, brings much more prosperity than buying a bottle of wine and sitting at home and consuming it.

Take, for example, that humble instrument the toothbrush. We have spent millions of dollars over the years selling toothbrushes and various kinds of tooth paste to the consumer. What have we succeeded in doing? We have conditioned 90 per cent of the people in America to brush their teeth. Not only is this a very good thing for the general health of the American people, but it also sells a lot of merchandise which, in turn, pays the wages of a lot of people. In short, it increases distribution, not only of these products, but of other products as well. There is no other country in the world where such a large percentage of the people brush their teeth regularly, and it's advertising that has conditioned people to do so.

The next factor in consumer conditioning is unpaid publicity that runs in newspapers, magazines, and can be heard on the radio and seen on television. The publishers of newspapers and magazines in the United States are thoroughly aware of the fact that their own prosperity and well-being are closely linked up with conditioning the consumer to buy merchandise. Consequently, they run hundreds of thousands of articles in the daily papers and magazines talking about things people should buy in order to live better, dress better, or feel better. This also is an American development that is only lately being copied abroad.

A good illustration of this is provided by the New York *Times* or the *Herald Tribune* any day in the week. There are articles about food, interior decoration, gardening, and, of course, about women's clothes. Every day in these great newspapers one sees many valuable inches of space freely devoted to pictures of the new clothes, accompanied by detailed descriptions of the styles that are being presented in the stores in New York City. Coats, suits, dresses, hats, shoes, stockings, handbags, and all the thousand-and-one things that a woman wants to buy are discussed and pictured there day after day. All of this is a very powerful way of informing the public and then conditioning the consumer to buy the new things, thereby helping to make obsolete the old.

Nowhere in the world are as many inches of newspaper space run without charge deliberately to promote all manner of things that the public can buy. Foreign newspapers generally feel that if anyone wants to say anything about a product that is for sale he should do it by buying advertising space. This, of course, is the selfish way of looking at it and perhaps makes more money for the paper, at least in the short run. But the enlightened attitude of American newspaper and magazine publishers toward helping to condition the public has been a major factor in moving enormous quantities of merchandise through the American mass-distribution system. Furthermore, these publishers are not just being altruistic. They know full well that this free publicity will eventually result in a lot more advertising revenue for them.

A third method of consumer conditioning is best labeled "showmanship." Hundreds of millions of dollars are spent each year on this.

One of the most common examples of showmanship in America is the fashion show. These are shows of new articles of apparel, generally feminine apparel, which are given constantly by all sorts of department stores and specialty stores, large and small. Millions of women flock to these shows every week of the year, which helps very much to condition these consumers to buy new clothes.

This is not an American invention, but it certainly is an American development. In addition to this, any number of lectures are given in hotels, in stores, even in museums, on new ideas in home decorating, how to make things, how to use medicines in order to stay thin, or avoid colds, or stay healthy, etc., etc. This type of showmanship also has an enormous effect on consumer conditioning and helps to move merchandise through mass-distribution channels.

One very effective piece of showmanship is demonstrated by many apparel stores and department stores several times a year. It is the bridal show. Lists of engaged girls are extracted from the daily newspapers, and invitations are sent to them. Advertisements also appear in the papers announcing the bridal fashion shows. It is not unusual to have several hundred girls and their mothers attend them. Bonwit Teller always jams its Bridal Department, which can seat approximately four hundred people. Many are actually turned away. A beautiful show is put on with live mannequins who show not only bridal gowns, but bridesmaids' dresses, lingerie, and other trousseau articles.

Some of these brides-to-be go to several stores before they make up their minds. Very often some sort of door prize is given, and the girls have to register as they come in to qualify for this. This is a way of obtaining the girls' names and addresses, as well as the time of the weddings, which can then be used later to solicit business.

Twice a year, when the new Paris clothes arrive, fashion shows are put on in many stores all over the country. These shows are almost always written up by the local newspapers and illustrated with photographs so that there is hardly a woman who can't find out what the new styles are and what she'll be wearing for the next season.

Twice a year at Bonwit Teller copies of these Paris styles are quickly made and first presented to the public in comprehensive fashion shows which hundreds of women attend. Then they are advertised in large ads in all the cities where Bonwit Teller operates stores.

Many fashion shows are given for charity. There is nothing that draws a capacity crowd more readily to a luncheon for some worthy local charity than a good fashion show. A committee of women who are working for a certain hospital, let us say, come in to see the head of the local department or specialty store and ask him to put on a fashion show at a luncheon or a tea that they are planning to give.

Very often members of the committee volunteer to model the clothes themselves which, from the store's point of view, is a very good idea because it gets these women into the store to try on the new clothes. It invariably happens that not only will many of them buy what they model in the show, but they will also buy other things that they saw while they were being fitted.

The committee then sells tickets to people who are interested in the hospital. The ticket not only includes the lunch, but also a large add-on which is a tax-deductible gift to the hospital.

This type of activity goes on in hundreds of stores all over the United States and illustrates how the consumer is quickly conditioned through showmanship so that she becomes very knowledgeable indeed. Naturally, it becomes more and more difficult to sell her last season's things, and alert stores must learn to dispose of them very rapidly in order to make place for the new fashion that the consumer is asking for.

Most store organizations have special crews that are

highly trained to give these fashion shows. They are given not only in the stores, but in hotels, women's clubs, and country clubs all over the United States.

Tiffany and Company developed a new type of showmanship that has become very popular, judging by the requests being received from women's organizations all over the country. This is a colored lantern-slide lecture on fashions in jewelry through the ages. This lecture starts with Egyptian jewelry, proceeds to Hellenistic, medieval, and Eastern jewelry, continues on to Benvenuto Cellini, Fabergé, and finally ends up with their own talented designer, Jean Schlumberger.

This lecture is given by their publicity director and is a rather inexpensive show to produce once the initial costs have been met. The cost of live mannequins and all the other expenses of a fashion show are avoided. All it requires is the lecturer and the lantern-slide operator.

This show has already appeared in Philadelphia, Pittsburgh, and Cleveland and is booked in various cities all over the country. It was first shown at The Metropolitan Museum of Art to a very enthusiastic audience.

Another form of showmanship that is often utilized is the so-called "publicity stunt." Many of these publicity stunts are ridiculous and bizarre as well as corny, but if well done, they are often effective in catching the consumer's attention and interesting her in new products of various kinds.

But the publicity stunt, although that is a poor word for the technique I am now going to describe, can be done in a dignified way and is often very constructive. Let me give you some examples.

On the first anniversary of Pearl Harbor, on December 7, 1942, which happened to be while I was president of Lord and Taylor, it occurred to me that we should commemorate the occasion by doing something to further the war effort. After thinking about it, I finally decided the only thing that would be in character for Lord and Taylor was to help the Government sell some war bonds.

I got my associates together and suggested to them that we should clear the entire main floor of all merchandise and sell nothing on the seventh of December but war bonds. Some of my associates were not too happy with this idea because they could visualize a considerable loss of business. But I convinced them that we were profiting pretty generously from the war and should do something patriotic in return. Besides, I argued, the publicity might perhaps be of considerable benefit to us.

So we prepared large, full-page advertisements and ran them in all the New York newspapers, announcing that all that would be sold on the main floor of Lord and Taylor on the morrow would be war bonds. When these advertisements hit the newsstands the next morning, they caused a sensation. No one had ever before cleared an entire main floor of all merchandise and devoted the space to a noncommercial, nonprofit endeavor of this kind. It was unique, to say the least. People came and literally gasped, and our main floor had more people on it that day than ever before in the store's history. Front-page stories appeared in practically all the newspapers across the country. For days afterward our business increased substantially because many people felt that we had sacrificed our commercial interests on the seventh of December to further our country's war effort. This is a good example of a "publicity stunt" that was constructive, dignified, and in character.

Another instance of showmanship occurred later on in the war when rumors were rife that clothing was going to be rationed in the same way that gasoline and certain foods had been. Our business at Lord and Taylor was fairly zooming, and this was true in all apparel stores across the country. It seemed as if rationing just had to come in order to keep some people from buying more clothing than they actually needed.

Consequently, I went to Washington to find out what the state of affairs actually was. I went to see my old friend Donald Nelson, whom I had known when he was a vice-president of Sears, Roebuck Company in Chicago. He was the head of the War Production Board in Washington. We talked the situation over and I did everything I could to dissuade him from putting through an executive order that would have placed clothing on the list of rationed goods.

While we were talking, he said to me, "By the way, we need a chairman of the Clothing Rationing Section. Will you take the job?" I thought for a minute and then realized that this would give me an inside seat that would permit me to influence the situation very much more than if I were just an outside spectator. I accepted his offer with the understanding that no announcement would be made that I would be the rationing chief and that it would be kept a deep, dark secret until and if it was necessary to do it. He then introduced me to the staff that would be under me and I spent the rest of the day getting acquainted with them and the statistical work that they had been doing.

On my way back to New York I racked by brain trying to figure out what could be done to forestall this move. I realized that rationing clothing would be a very much more difficult proposition than rationing gasoline or sugar. And there was no telling what would happen if the bureaucrats got their feet in the door in this complicated and sensitive industry. I was determined to prevent it if I could. Finally I hit upon an idea that I thought might stop the buying splurge, and I knew that if this could be done there would be no reason for clothing rationing.

When I got back to New York, I got my advertising staff together and we prepared full-page ads that read as follows:

We wager $5,000 that there will be no clothes rationing. If we lose we will pay the $5,000 to the U.S.O. But we do not think we will lose because we are very close to the authorities in Washington and we can positively say that there is no present intention of rationing clothing.

The next morning we broke with these ads in all the New York papers, and they were reproduced free of charge in many papers all over the United States. The papers picked it up with front-page stories as well as editorials. And wonder of wonders, the frantic buying of clothing stopped overnight and went back to normal.

The next day Don Nelson called me from Washington and said, "Say, Walter. I think you've done yourself out of a job. The reports I'm getting from around the country indicate that there's not going to be any need for rationing since you ran those ads."

This publicity stunt again redounded to the enormous benefit of Lord and Taylor even though our business was adversely affected by the decrease in panic buying. But we were just as happy about that because we were getting plenty of business in any case.

This publicity stunt was a reverse English one. Instead of increasing our business, which, of course, is generally the objective of publicity, it decreased our business, but the resultant good will we built was beyond price.

Here is another example of the use of showmanship through a "publicity stunt." This one was by Tiffany and Company.

One of Tiffany's customers ordered a gold putter, which was to be presented to an individual on a certain anniversary, and it occurred to me that some good publicity might be gotten from such an unusual present. So we photographed the putter and subsequently ran an ad about it.

We decided to do a deadpan type of ad in the *Wall Street Journal* describing the putter in very somber tones as "Tiffany's fourteen-carat solid gold putter at $1,475." At the bottom we gagged the following line that often appears in financial ads in the *Wall Street Journal* in small type. "This advertisement appears for the record only because the entire stock has been sold." We dropped the ad into the paper without making any comment to the press or issuing any press releases.

The next day all hell broke loose. All the wire services and the newspapers called us up and wanted to know all about it. How many had we made, how many had we sold, etc., etc.

But the unexpected happened in that we also heard from the United States Mint, which called up and said this was a most disturbing idea. It had received complaints from the Canadian government, among others. Almost every sporting-goods manufacturer in the country had called them up and asked for a license to make gold putters, gold baseball bats, gold footballs, etc., and in view of the current drain on our gold supply, they were very wrought up indeed. When we explained that we were, of course, within the law in that this putter was sold for presentation purposes only and was being made only to order, they agreed that what we were doing was all right provided we didn't go into mass production, which hardly seemed likely at $1,475. For days, weeks, and months clippings came in from all over the United States, Europe, South America, even as far away as Hong Kong, headlining the fact that Tiffany's had offered a solid-gold putter for $1,475. We even made some of the Soviet papers, which was interesting, even though we had to admit that the market there for gold putters was probably somewhat restricted. A great many people came in, not only to see the gold putter, but also to buy other things while they were in the store.

So there is no question that showmanship is important in moving merchandise through the channels of distribution. But the showmanship must be tailored to the situation and must be in character with the organization that uses it.

CONSUMER CONDITIONING

The fourth method of conditioning consumers is through *display*.

The technique of display divides itself into two parts, *window display* and *interior display*.

Let us examine window display first.

Window display has become almost a fine art in America. Nowhere else in the world has the ingenuity and inventiveness of America's foremost window display artists even been approached. Only on the Rue St. Honoré and occasionally on New Bond Street in London is anything comparable being done, and that is not very often. But all over America one sees fine window displays that are frequently changed as the various selling seasons progress.

I believe everyone will admit that there is no comparable show in the world equal to the remarkable windows that one sees every day of the year on Fifth Avenue in New York. People come from all over just to walk up and down Fifth Avenue and enjoy this great sight.

Some years ago, when I was with Lord and Taylor, I put in the first window display on Fifth Avenue that was entirely devoid of merchandise. Every window was filled with huge gold bells that swung back and forth against a bright red background. Muted loud-speakers had been installed three stories above the street so that these Christmas bells could be heard as well as seen. It created a sensation and drew enormous crowds of people to view them. I told a friend of mine that I actually saw some people looking at the windows with tears streaming down their faces. At this he quipped, rather unkindly I thought, "Was it before they went into the store or was it after they came out?"

In my opinion the peer of all display directors is Gene Moore, who runs the staff of twenty-three people who do the Bonwit Teller and Tiffany windows. The taste, the imagination, and the creativeness that are so consistently maintained by Mr. Moore and his staff are one of the truly remarkable accomplishments in the entire display world.

When I became the head of Tiffany and Company, I asked Mr. Moore if he would also like to do the Tiffany windows as well as those of Bonwit Teller. He was delighted. While discussing the matter, he asked me what instructions I had for him. I said, "First of all, don't try to sell anything. Leave that to us. Your job is just to make these windows the most beautiful in the world."

And he has.

Consequently, the now-famous Tiffany windows draw people from everywhere. Some people even keep track of when they are changed so they can come down to see what astonishing things Mr. Moore has done.

Display also functions as a consumer conditioner within a store. *Interior display* is very important because it affects the consumer at the "point of sale," so to speak. This is also a highly professional technique and has a very powerful influence on the consumer. Well-constructed interior displays will sell much more merchandise than poorly done ones. It is not a function that should be left to amateurs because it requires a real professional to do it properly.

Interior display, in my view, divides itself into two

techniques, neither of which is very well understood. One I call the "idea display," and the other one I call the "assortment display."

Let us take up the idea display first. This concerns itself with projecting an idea about the merchandise displayed. In other words, it should be an arrangement of merchandise that projects a style point or a fashion point or a cohesive idea to the consumer. Let us say that the display staff wants to get over the idea of taste and imagination in table settings, as has been done by Tiffany and Company for the last several years. Here's how this was accomplished.

First it was decided to invite a group of twelve New York hostesses, all of whom were known for their great taste and originality, to do twelve table settings exactly as they would set them for dinner and luncheon parties in their own homes. These were followed up during the next spring season by a group of tables done by well-known New York interior decorators, who used Tiffany merchandise for table settings and brought in their own tables, chairs, linens, and other decorative objects.

This program has been consistently followed for three years with great success. Newspapers and magazines give it a great deal of space and attention and people come in large numbers to see the settings. They have put over the idea of how to use imagination and taste in setting tables for breakfast, luncheon, and dinner, and it has, of course, had a very good effect on Tiffany's business, too.

The assortment display consists of showing the entire assortment of a certain category of merchandise so that the customer can see at a glance what the selection is. I experimented with this first many years ago when I was a vice-president of R. H. Macy & Co. One case comes to my mind.

I took all the thimbles in the notion department and arranged them on a board in one of the display cases. There were more than 130 different thimbles. I merely lined them up like tin soldiers with a small price and description under each one. My recollection is that the thimble business increased more than 250 per cent after this display was installed in the department. It was also an enormous timesaver for the clerks. Similar assortment displays were installed in other departments in the store, and wherever this was done sales increased commensurately.

All one has to do is go into any good drugstore in almost any town in America to see how much time and thought have been put on the assortment displays. Many of these displays are devised by the manufacturers themselves, and display fixtures are either sold or given to the drugstore. In the average cosmetic department in a department store every lineal foot has been carefully studied. The arrangement of the displays has all been pretested and studied to find out exactly the right arrangement that will appeal to the most customers and sell the most goods.

Grocery stores often utilize the services of a person known in the trade as a "rack jobber." He is particularly in evidence today because of the present-day tendency to carry merchandise other than food. He operates in the field of small housewares or hosiery, cleaning supplies, etc., which the grocery-store manager doesn't know much about and hasn't got the time to take care of.

The rack jobber puts in a display fixture containing merchandise that has been carefully studied and scientifically arranged. He then services this fixture by keeping the merchandise in stock through a model stock plan that he has developed.

Most of these racks have been very ingeniously built so as to get the maximum attention from the passer-by. And the rack is often moved from one place to another in the store until just the right place is found where the maximum business seems to result.

"Yes, "display" in all its ramifications plays a most important part in the four arts of conditioning the consumer to buy more merchandise, namely, advertising, publicity, showmanship, and display.

CHAPTER

8

FASHION

The seventh important principle in mass distribution is the element of *fashion*.

The word "fashion," unfortunately, has been rather loosely and indiscriminately used as a synonym for style, design, or just women's clothes in general. And this, I'm afraid, has greatly confused the situation. Let us, therefore, start by defining a few terms.

In order to define the word "fashion," you first have to define the word "style" because one follows the other. Style is a characteristic way of expressing something or doing something.

FASHION

It may be a style of speaking, such as the Oxford accent, a style of composing music, such as Bach. It may be a style of painting, such as Impressionism, or a group of designs, say in shoes, that all have pointed toes. The style in that instance is pointed toes.

It may be the length of the skirt, or a silhouette; or a style in furniture such as Chippendale; or it may be the oratorical style of a speaker such as Winston Churchill.

Fashion, however, strictly speaking, is the acceptance of a style by enough people.

For example, if enough people accept the style of pointed toes, then that becomes the fashion. If enough Englishmen speak with an Oxford accent, that is the fashion in that particular group. If enough people decide to follow a style set by Balenciaga of knee-length skirts, or skirts halfway down the calf, it would become the fashion. In other words, fashion has to do with the acceptance of a characteristic way of doing things or a characteristic way of designing by enough people, or by a group of people sometimes thought to be "discriminating." If a style in women's clothes is accepted by a small group of well-dressed women, then it becomes what is called "high fashion."

Confusion arises because other common usages of the word fashion are rather broad. Sometimes the word is used simply to mean women's clothes. Sometimes Bonwit Teller says, for example, that it sells fashion. It means that the store sells clothes that are acceptable to discriminating women and are, in its opinion, good style.

Fashion, obviously, exerts a very strong influence on

the style a manufacturer produces or the designs his designing department turns out. It would be very dangerous for him to design things without giving heed to this element of fashion. It is a very foolish manufacturer who plans his products without getting advice from distribution people who understand fashion.

Fashion is one of the most powerful economic elements in the whole distribution cycle. If there were no fashion, and it's hard to conceive of such a thing, all products would be standardized as the Mother Hubbard used to be, and as overalls for young people are today. Without fashion there would be a catastrophic decline in business.

But of course there is no way to escape fashion and its tremendous power to make millions of jobs and influence the economy. Let me give you one or two examples of how powerful that influence has been in the past.

America's Northwest was explored and settled because trappers went out and trapped beavers. Beaver fur was selling at the time for very high prices in London at the beginning of the nineteenth century. Trappers pushed on west as the beaver was exterminated to satisfy the great demand that existed in England.

Why was it in such demand? Simply because a certain gentleman called Beau Brummell made a wager of a thousand guineas that if he walked down Piccadilly in a ridiculous hat, even one that looked like a stovepipe, everyone would want to emulate him. He would set the fashion, and men would want to wear stovepipe hats from then on. Silly and trivial as this sounds, he won his bet and what he said would happen did. All the so-called smart men and dandies in London rushed out to buy stovepipe hats. Inasmuch as these hats were made of beaver fur, the impact was felt in the American Northwest and in western Canada where the trappers braved the elements, perished in blizzards, and explored the country in order to find beaver fur.

Thus, Mr. Brummell, by simply walking down Piccadilly with a most peculiar contraption on his head, exerted a powerful influence on the opening up of the entire Northwest.

Another example goes all the way back to ancient Rome. A great many people, particularly historians, feel that ancient Rome fell because the Romans drank too much, lived dissolute lives, and neglected their duties. Undoubtedly that had a lot to do with it. But in addition to these things there was something else that exerted a strong influence, and that was the fashion in men's clothes.

The fashionable way to dress in Rome was to wear a toga. And any old toga was not good enough. The great Roman patricians and senators had to have their togas made of silk. Cotton wasn't good enough. Linen wasn't good enough. They had to be of silk. That was the fashion.

Where did the silk come from? It came from China. It was brought over by the great overland caravans that crossed the desert bringing bales of silk that took months and months to go from China to the Mediterranean Sea and were then shipped by galley on to Rome. Money to pay for the silk went back on the return trip with orders for more bales of silk so that the Roman snobs could have their silk togas, which were the fashion.

While the Roman legions were conquering Gaul and the rest of Europe, they sent vast treasures, including gold, back to Rome. So there was plenty of money to send to China to pay for the silk togas. But after a while the conquests stopped and very little gold came into Rome. Now you would think that the Romans would have been prudent enough to stop sending so much gold to China for silk, and would start using cotton togas or togas made of other materials. But that was not the case. If you think they were that sensible, you simply under-estimate the power of fashion. They still wanted their fashionable silk togas. So they continued to ship gold to China until the gold was practically gone. Thus one of the economic reasons for the fall of Rome was that they just plain ran out of money. Moral—never under-estimate the power of fashion.

Many examples in modern times illustrate clearly how powerful the element of fashion is in mass distribution. Twice a year thousands of buyers flock to Paris during the fashion openings to see what the great couture houses such as Dior, Balenciaga, Lanvin, Ricci, Jacques Heim, and the others are going to do to women's clothes. Hundreds of thousands of dollars are spent in cables and despatches to newspapers and magazines all over the world that print thousands of pages describing what these new fashions are.

Then the great ready-to-wear houses, particularly in

the United States, which employ hundreds of thousands of people, get busy making adaptations and copies based on these new silhouettes, new necklines, hem lengths, details, etc. Their customers eagerly await these new styles.

Millions of yards of materials are turned out, based on the designs, types, and colors introduced by these Paris designers. All of this creates an enormous amount of new business, supports millions of people not only in manufacturing jobs but in advertising, publishing, retailing, wholesaling, transportation, and every other facet of the economic system. These designs make obsolete much that went before, which means that millions of women have to discard clothes that are no longer in fashion and would make them feel dowdy should they wear them.

This element of obsolescence in fashion is a very important factor in mass distribution. Years and years ago there was very much less of it and a woman could wear a dress for many seasons simply by letting it out if she had put on a little extra weight, or taking it in if she got thinner. But not nowadays, at least not in the Western world. In the communist world, however, it is entirely different. The element of fashion there is very much less important and consequently all the Russian women wear their clothes for years, which explains why they all look so old-fashioned to Western eyes.

Style, of course, by no means confines itself to women's clothes. It is increasingly more important today in everything. In men's clothes, for example, shoulders and trousers have become narrower of late years. Vests have lately returned to fashion. Bowler hats, some of rather dubious hues, are again seen after many years of being out of fashion. The hard sennit straw is again popular in America in the summertime, though it went out of fashion years ago and the so-called Nassau straw hat was the only one worn for a long time. Men's shoes have changed from rather staple styles, wing tips, etc., which were in fashion for many years, to the softer and more informal "Italian" type of shoe.

Fashion in automobiles has also been changing. Some years ago people would have only the black, sleek car. Then the manufacturers changed to a rather ugly two-tone job that found many critics, but also a great many buyers, and boosted the automobile business substantially. Now fashion in automobiles is again changing, and the smaller car is becoming more popular. In five years the smaller foreign car has jumped from about 1 per cent of the American market to about 10 per cent. The big American automobile companies have begun to meet this competition by putting out their own smaller cars in order to keep up with this change in fashion.

Sometimes the style that becomes the fashion is not always in good taste. It's been my observation, however, that in the long run the styles that are in better taste, generally speaking, are longer in fashion than those that are ugly. The two-tone car is a case in point. The single-color car was in fashion much longer than the two-tone style. The latter lasted only a few years and is now becoming unpopular.

Good style in women's clothes also seems to be more enduring than bad style. Taste is not the only idea a woman has in mind when she purchases her new clothes. Very often she feels she must emphasize her attractiveness for the benefit of the opposite sex. Her personal interpretation of this may not always be in good taste.

Taste, of course, concerns itself not only with a dress, a coat, or a hat, as individual things, but it also concerns itself with a proper combination of all of them. A woman may buy several items, all of which may be individually attractive, but when she puts them on they may not go together at all. Then, again, taste determines that there is a time and place for everything, and the clothes a woman wears must be suitable to the occasion and to the time of day. This, however, is not always properly observed.

As a matter of fact, one constantly sees women in the morning in dresses that are suitable only for the late afternoon, or hats that are full of sequins that might perhaps be in good taste for cocktails, but certainly not for shopping or for luncheon.

The same thing, of course, is true in *décor*. The objects in a room may all be individually very attractive and in good style, but they may not go together, and the room as an ensemble may turn out to be very bad indeed.

Perhaps we should stop a minute and define taste. Taste is the power of *discerning* and *appreciating* beauty, order, and proportion. It also means that things that are used together must be suitable to each other. Taste is the ability to judge whether the lines in a design are harmonious and in proportion, whether a design has character, is sincere or false. A design has a personality and may be judged very much as a person is judged. A good design is alive, never dull, and has a definite purpose in life. The colors, too, must be harmonious and have an objective. They must be there for some definite reason, not just thrown together in a haphazard way. Taste takes real knowledge. It takes a background of culture and, above all, a real interest in good design and good style. Contrary to popular opinion, however, it *can* be acquired.

Flair, on the other hand, often confused with taste, is an entirely different thing. Flair is the *instinctive* and *intuitive* ability to do things in an unusual way, either in designing something, in saying something, or in doing something. A dinner party can be given with flair if it is unusual, gay, and entertaining instead of just like every other dinner party. Flair is the creative element. No designer can be really great without flair. Nor can a speaker be a great orator without flair.

If flair and taste are combined there is the unusual intuitive creative element on one hand plus the knowledge, the discernment, and the judgment to guide it on the other. Then the result may be a Michelangelo, a Palladio, or a Balenciaga.

These attributes are becoming more and more necessary in the business world today, and the people who have these qualities are going to be in greater and greater demand as the public's taste improves.

Most people, however, are lazy about taste. They like

to feel either they were born with it, or they have the discernment and judgment about artistic things through intuition. Nothing could be further from the truth.

Taste is something you must work for. You have to expose yourself to good things and cultivate people who have taste.

There are lots of good courses given in design schools and museums nowadays. Knowledge and background can be acquired and after diligent work will eventually result in taste. Of course the person who has a real flair for the artistic has an obvious advantage provided he goes to work and acquires the knowledge necessary to develop his taste.

Students of fashion, and there are many in the distribution field, are constantly alert to see which way it is going. It is a very difficult and tricky element in the distribution cycle. If you guess wrong on fashion you can lose literally millions of dollars. Great care is always taken by merchandisers and manufacturers not only to keep abreast of fashion but to prognosticate its future. It is probably the most difficult single element in the distribution picture. The vagaries of fashion and the fickleness of some women make it extremely difficult accurately to forecast what is going to happen next in the field of fashion.

The public, however, wouldn't be interested in products if they were not varied from year to year. It is the element of new design and new style that intrigues and makes it interested in buying new things or variations of old things.

If it weren't for the element of fashion in the Western world the number of jobs in factories, as well as in stores, would be much fewer. There would be very little hope of supporting our present prosperity if things were as staple and dull as the goods are in Soviet Russia.

9

THE BANK CHECK

The eighth pillar on which distribution rests is the practice of *payment by check*.

In America, we are so used to paying bills by check that it may not occur to us that this is an important keystone in mass distribution. It seems so simple, so everyday, and so unimportant. Actually it is not unimportant, it is of paramount importance. Without the bank check, mass distribution simply could not proceed.

The interesting thing is that only in the United States is there any large-scale paying of bills by check. England comes second in quantity, but the number of checks per capita used in England is very much less than in the United States.

The American habit of payment of personal bills by check, outside of a few large cities in Europe, doesn't exist in the rest of the world. There the bank check is used almost exclusively by business concerns and commercial people. The average consumer has no such thing as a checking account at his local bank.

Even in this country, it is amazing to note how many people come to stores and pay their bills in cash. On income-tax day, too, thousands of people line up at the Internal Revenue offices and pay their income taxes in cash. Cash, however, is the *only* thing used by consumers in Asia, Africa, South America, China, India, Russia, and in many parts of Europe. In some places they use the barter system, which is even more cumbersome and slow.

What's wrong with paying in cash? Isn't it better to have cash in hand than to have a bank check which might perhaps "bounce"? The only thing wrong with paying in cash is that there just isn't enough currency in any country in the world to support large-scale mass distribution.

If most transactions were not paid for by check in the United States, we would have to inflate our currency by a fantastic percentage to do business. Even if we did that, the loss of time spent running around to pay for things in cash would slow up the whole system so much we would have to settle for a lower standard of living.

The bank check is a marvelous little invention. It

makes it possible to pay for all the transactions that are necessary to keep up the high level of business activity in the U.S.A. It is a very important pillar in mass distribution, and without it mass distribution would not be possible.

Even in a big city such as Paris, very few people pay their bills by check. If a woman buys some clothes, say at the house of Dior, she gives her chauffeur the exact amount in French francs and sends him down to Dior's to pay for it in cash. She wouldn't dream of paying by check. Chances are she hasn't even got a checking account.

A little article in a French newspaper says, "The era of the overstuffed wallet seems to be going out of fashion in France. Payment by check is becoming more popular than it used to be. This is largely due to a publicity campaign that the French banks have been waging to break down the *suspicion* and *ridicule* normally attached in France to the idea of paying bills by check."

This may sound incredible to one who is used to paying his bills with a bank check, but it is true. It is almost unheard of for a consumer on the continent of Europe to pay her bills by writing checks and mailing them to her creditors.

In many countries money is hoarded in cellars or attics or other silly places which, of course, keeps the money immobile. In America we keep it in the bank, which means that the money is always in circulation, being constructively used to undergird mass production and distribution.

I have always advised merchants in the United States

and abroad to be alert to this important keystone of distribution, and cooperate with their local banks in getting more and more people to use checking accounts. It is good for their own business if they can get their customers to do this. You can statistically relate the business in any given city to its circulation of personal bank checks.

In my opinion this whole idea of checking accounts and payment by check has not been sufficiently stressed by businessmen even in the United States, and certainly not abroad. It takes a long time to generate the habit.

People for many years were suspicious of banks because repeated bank panics closed them and they lost their money. The last time this happened in the United States was in 1933 when millions of dollars were lost by consumers who had their money in banks that closed and were never opened again. Then we finally passed some much-needed laws creating the Federal Deposit Insurance Corporation, and now nobody in this country is afraid to keep his money in a bank. This is most important, because without this assurance the present level of mass distribution would not be possible.

I cannot understand why this important keystone in the distribution system has been so generally overlooked abroad. There should be more effort made to popularize the importance of payment by check.

The other day I happened to be looking at the annual report of the Bank of America in the State of California. They have more than 7,000,000 checking accounts. There are approximately 11,000,000 people in the state of California, and this one bank has more than 7,000,000, accounts. So if you include all the other banks in California I believe you will find more checking accounts in the state of California than there are people. This, of course, means that some people and certainly some corporations have more than one bank account.

But let me illustrate the very wide use of the bank check in the United States with a few statistics. The number of checking accounts in insured commercial banks rose from 22,100,000 in 1936 to 54,400,000 in 1959. Thus in 1959 nearly one out of every two persons, twenty-one years or older, owned a checking account, whereas in 1936 it was only one out of four.

The growing practice of paying wages by check has also contributed to the use of checking accounts by lower-income families. A recent survey showed that the percentage of companies paying hourly wages by check increased from 69 per cent in 1937 to 82 per cent in 1954. This is good because it encourages people to open checking accounts. But only in America is this true.

I don't know how a movement can be started abroad to get more people to have bank accounts. There doesn't seem to be the slightest interest in most of the countries in Europe, and certainly not in Asia, Africa, or South America. Nevertheless, it is true that if more bank accounts are not opened so that the lowly check can become an important instrument of payment, mass distribution isn't going to develop there. And of course if mass distribution doesn't develop, then mass production won't succeed either.

Every once in a while we see a story in an American newspaper about the death of a hermit in whose house large quantities of currency were found. This, however, is so unusual that it almost always makes the front page. The usual practice in this counrty is to keep your money in a bank and to pay bills by check.

This habit is growing all the time and now banks offer special checking accounts that require no balances. The depositor merely pays a small service charge and 10 cents for the privilege of using the checking facilities of the bank. Such special checking accounts, of course, can grow into regular accounts as the person involved gains in affluence.

Another innovation that has lately been offered is a credit checking account. In this case, the customer goes to the bank and arranges a credit of, let's say, $500, and gets a checkbook authorizing him to draw against this credit. At the same time, he agrees to deposit a certain amount of money against this loan each month. This enables him to draw checks without having any money in the bank at all, simply by being in debt to the bank for the agreed-upon amount.

All of these things are constructive, in my opinion, because they increase the use of the bank check. Not only does this mean that there is less cash around the house in case one is robbed, but more important, from my point of view, it helps to speed up payment for merchandise which is so essential in order to have a vigorous and growing distribution system.

In order to get an idea of the volume of money involved, let us take a look at the figures. Last year more than $900,000,000,000 changed hands through the use of the bank check. There is no country in the world where such an amount of money and so many different checking transactions are handled.

This, of course, has a direct bearing on the volume of distribution in this country. It is pretty hard to figure out which is the chicken and which is the egg, but if distribution were less, the bank checks would be less, and if the bank checks were more, the distribution would also be more. One is a measure of the other.

Some people say that it is risky to accept checks, and naturally there is some risk. But it can be minimized if the transaction is intelligently handled. For example, no well-run store will accept a check for a larger amount than the transaction itself. This is the best way to put through a quick fraud. The average check passer uses this trick constantly. He goes into a store and buys something for, say, $15.00. He gives the clerk a check for $25.00 and asks to have the merchandise sent to a phony address. He waits for the $10.00 change leaves the store, and that's the last they see of him.

Some sales clerks fall for this and put the transaction through. The merchandise arrives at the phony address, is returned, and the check bounces. However, if the check is for the same amount as the merchandise and is sent to a name and address, you at least can trace the transaction. If the check bounces, the merchandise comes back and nothing except time has been lost.

But in the retail business we find that a very large majority of people are honest, and reasonable precaution can keep the losses from bad checks down to a minimum. As a matter of fact, in a large organization such as

Bonwit Teller, doing more than $39,000,000 worth of business a year, the bad checks don't amount to more than $3,000 a year. This is certainly not a very sizable amount.

I had an interesting experience some years ago that demonstrated how honest people in this country are about bank checks. It happened in 1933, just after President Roosevelt came into office and closed the banks. I was then an officer of Montgomery Ward and Company in Chicago. Within three or four days we received orders for merchandise containing checks that amounted to more than $45,000,000. The banks were closed, and we knew that some of them would never reopen again. Our problem was what to do about it.

If we didn't send the merchandise, we faced another problem. New merchandise was constantly arriving at our mail-order plants, and unless merchandise went out to customers, we would soon be completely swamped.

I also felt that the people who had sent in $45,000,000 worth of bank checks were generally honest people who had been dealing with us for years, and we should take the business risk and send them the merchandise they had ordered. So I proposed to our board of directors that we print a statement that would say as follows:

Since we received your order your bank has closed. We feel, however, that you are in need of this merchandise so we are sending it to you herewith and are enclosing your bank check in this package. We would appreciate it if you would send us currency, money orders, or stamps in payment of this merchandise.

Sincerely,
MONTGOMERY WARD

Well, the board of directors almost had a fit. Some of the conservative bankers on the board estimated that we would lose almost the entire $45,000,000. The treasurer of the company estimated that the loss would certainly amount to $15,000,000, and I calculated it would cost us about $1,000,000.

I argued, however, that it was worth $1,000,000 to show these people that we trusted them. Anyway, I felt it was absolutely necessary to keep merchandise flowing out while new merchandise was flowing in, because if we didn't, the glut would cost us a great deal more than $1,000,000 in markdowns and handling charges.

We argued for three days, and I finally won my point. I rushed out and had the letter I quoted above printed. Then we began to ship merchandise like mad.

It is true the money took a little while to come in because many of the banks in the farm areas never opened their doors. But it kept on coming, and the amazing part of it was that at the end of six months our total loss amounted to the incredibly small sum of $15,000. We could hardly believe it. The figures were checked and double-checked, and that was the total. I have told this story to many people and they have all looked at me with astonishment. They just can't believe that out of $45,000,000 we lost only $15,000.

This gave me great faith in the American people and has always made me feel that with very few exceptions they are honest. Consequently, when some years later I opened the Boston branch of Bonwit Teller I tried another experiment that also tested the honesty of the American people.

We had only 3,000 charge accounts in the Boston area. In order to do enough business to break even we had to have 30,000 charge accounts, so I decided to open a charge account for everyone who came in. We didn't advertise this because if we had, naturally some crooks would have responded. We merely did it. And we did it until we got our 30,000 charge accounts.

I recall the first day a man tried to buy a bottle of perfume for $10.00. The clerk would not take his money. He couldn't understand it. I thought she probably wasn't explaining it very well because she was new, so I stepped up and explained what we were doing. He listened carefully, nodded his head, and said, "I think it's a very good idea. I admire your courage, too. But I wish you would make an exception in my case because there are some things you don't want on the record." I laughed, turned to the clerk, and said, "Take the gentleman's money."

How much money did we lose in this case? I had set up a reserve of $30,000 because it would have cost $1.00 to get charge references on each account. But we didn't have time to do this. So inasmuch as we were saving $1.00 apiece on these 30,000 accounts I put up the $30,000 as a reserve. I didn't know whether this would be enough or not, but I figured it wouldn't be any less because after all most of these people were people we had not done business with before, and it was fair to assume there would be some dead beats among them.

However, we were all astonished when the direct loss amounted to only $54.00. In addition to this, we lost $2,000 more through bad credit risks. But this was about normal, even if we had looked up every account in the regular way. It illustrated again that Americans are "money honest."

I hope I have demonstrated that you can't have mass distribution without a wide use of the bank check. And until countries all over the world begin to understand this, they are simply fooling themselves by building more and more factories to step up their production machinery, because their distribution facilities will not keep up with their production facilities. Certainly one thing they must do in order to step up their distribution machinery is to encourage a very wide use of the bank check.

10

THE PRINCIPLE OF
POST-CONSUMPTION SAVING

The ninth principle that underlies mass distribution is *post-consumption saving*.

That sounds like a mysterious phrase, but it simply means saving your money after you've spent it. In other words, it is just the opposite of what most people do when they put their money into a savings bank. To do that you have to save it first. But in post-consumption saving you buy the merchandise first and then commit yourself to save and pay for it later.

This principle of post-consumption saving is very, very

important because human beings, being human, find it much easier to save their money *after* they have committed themselves to buy something. It takes a lot more character to resolve to save your money ahead of time and put it into a savings bank.

The statistics, of course, also bear this out. The amount of installment credit extended during 1959 was much larger than the personal savings that went into saving banks in the same time. The personal savings amounted to $24,000,000,000, whereas people were committed to $48,000,000,000 on the installment plan. The fact that people found it easier to save their money after they bought the merchandise they wanted is what I call post-consumption saving.

There has always been a great hue and cry against selling things on the installment plan. There are those who say it is terrible to encourage people to go into debt. But in my opinion there is nothing basically wrong with installment credit. The consumer polices himself remarkably well. Generally he is pretty farsighted about how much he should spend.

Of course there are people who get into trouble. But then some people always get into trouble. But most manage their obligations very well. It is interesting to note that in the depth of the depression of the 1930's the repossession of goods that had been bought on the installment plan never exceeded 2 per cent in any one year.

Actually, I feel very strongly that we should encourage credit selling. I feel it is one of the most important instruments in creating mass distribution without which it would be impossible to move the goods that we produce in the United States today.

There is another kind of post-consumption saving that generally doesn't extend itself so far into the future. That is the thirty-day charge account that is so generally used in this country and in England. On the continent of Europe, however, it is much less popular and, of course, in the rest of the world it is almost unheard of.

There is no other country in the world where the charge account is as widely used as it is in the United States. As far as I know, it is another American invention. The charge account is a most powerful influence in getting people to buy more merchandise, and I can only reiterate that buying more merchandise makes more jobs and creates more prosperity. If you distribute less merchandise, of course, it simply follows as night the day that you will have fewer jobs and a lower average prosperity than we now have.

When Mr. Christian Dior, the great French designer, was here about a year before he died, I took him on a tour through Bonwit Teller. Surprisingly enough, he spent most of his time in our credit department. He was fascinated. He wanted to know all about the operation. He asked dozens of questions. Then he turned to me and said, "You know, we don't have any charge accounts at Dior."

I replied, "Really? I thought you did. My recollection is that my wife has gotten bills from Dior whenever she has bought things there."

"Oh, yes," he said, "we send bills, but we don't run any charge accounts. If a woman comes in and buys a handbag, we send her a bill. If she buys a dress, we send her another bill. And if she comes in and buys a coat, we send her a third bill. And then she sends her chauffeur down with cash to pay them. French people never use checks, you know."

Then he instructed his assistant, who was with him, to come back and study our system of handling charge accounts to see whether they couldn't introduce it into their operation in Paris.

A store such as Bonwit Teller normally does about 80 per cent of its total business with charge accounts. Less expensive stores, departments stores, etc., of course, have smaller percentages. And then there are the cash stores such as the A. & P. and others, which have, up to this point, not gone into it very deeply. They are, however, studying it, and I believe the time will come when you will be able to charge food in most of the food chains in this country.

Another development of the last few years is a phase of post-consumption saving known as revolving credit. There are various plans, but one of the most common is this: you establish credit with a store, let's say $100 and then you can buy up to $100 worth of merchandise. You are supposed to pay down a third of that each month, and as you pay it, you can keep adding more purchases so that the amount you owe always stays roughly around the $100 mark.

These revolving credits are becoming more and more popular because there are a great many people who don't want to commit themselves to pay within thirty days for fear they will not have enough money to take care of their obligations at the end of the month. By being able to spread them over a three- or four-month period it makes it very much easier to budget.

Lately there has been a tremendous development in credit plans run by outside credit organizations. One of the first in this field was the Diners' Club, which has been very successful and does an enormous amount of business. They discovered that very few restaurants extended credit to their patrons, so they entered this field and offered a credit card that was good in thousands of restaurants all over this country and also in Europe. They arranged with all these restaurants to honor their credit cards in return for a charge running up to approximately 7 per cent to the restaurant. This meant that a man could walk into almost any restaurant in this country or abroad and simply show his credit card, sign the check, and it is all charged on the account and mailed to him each month by the Diners' Club.

Since then others have gotten into the field, notably the American Express Company, which has gone beyond the restaurant and hotel field to credit arrangements with various merchants. The same thing has been done in New York by the Chase Manhattan Bank, and the movement is growing by leaps and bounds.

One problem I feel they are going to have trouble with, which some of them largely overlooked, is the fact when people buy merchandise they are sometimes dissatisfied with it and bring it back for credit or exchange. This is a headache to most stores because a good deal of paper work is necessary to credit the merchandise and put this credit on the customer's bill. Sometimes the merchandise is bought in one month and credited the next month, which means that the customer doesn't see the credit appear on his or her bill and very often inquires about it. She has forgotten that she credited this merchandise in the next month, so it will appear on her next month's bill. She doesn't like to pay a bill for merchandise that she has subsequently credited and stores are constantly making adjustments to straighten out these accounts.

But when the transaction is charged to a customer's account, say with the American Express Company, and later credited, the amount of red tape necessary to straighten out the transaction from the customer to the American Express, from the American Express to the store involved, and then back again through the cycle is enormous and is causing some severe operating headaches.

I don't know whether these organizations can iron this out, but I do think they're going to have a great deal of trouble with it.

Nevertheless, all this illustrates the extension of the credit idea which is so enormously important in creating a climate for mass distribution. In my opinion, the more credit wisely extended, the more distribution.

One effect of this use of credit is that the family that has committed itself generally finds it necessary to deprive itself of other enjoyments or pleasure in order to meet its obligations. It is my opinion that one reason alcoholic consumption has gone down is because the husband hesitates to stop in at the corner saloon for a drink with the boys when he knows his wife is waiting for his pay check so they can make their payments on their installment accounts. If they don't the car may be repossessed or they may lose that washing machine, all of which they have found are pretty necessary.

This kind of discipline, which is a result of post-consumption saving, is a good thing. It makes for more careful, orderly planning and budgeting and less impulsive spending on liquor or other foolish things.

Another important element in the post-consumption saving field is the automobile credit company, such as the General Motors Acceptance Corporation and C.I.T. They finance automobile paper. For many years the commercial banks missed their opportunities in this field, but they have lately gone into it. Now it is possible to go to your own bank and arrange to buy your car on the installment plan, having the payments deducted from your bank account each month.

It goes without saying that this country could not, under any circumstances, sell 6,000,000 cars a year unless a great many of them were sold on the installment plan. It is hardly conceivable that distribution can grow in other parts of the world to sizable proportions without this element of post-consumption saving.

The credit systems that have grown up in this country have not been developed quickly. It takes a great deal of time and it takes a great deal of education. Nevertheless, it is important that a start be made in this direction, and the more positive steps that can be taken, the better.

Foolish propaganda about how bad it is to buy on the installment plan will not help. Russia, up until quite recently would not permit it. But within the last few months they have begun to permit people to buy on the installment plan. This is the first glimmer that I have seen of any consciousness on the part of the Soviet bureaucracy that if they're going to get an improvement in distribution they've got to begin to utilize the tools that are necessary to make distribution work.

The important tool I have outlined in this chapter is the credit tool in all its various phases. Post-consumption saving is one of the potent factors in mass distribution, and the growth of mass distribution around the world can be no faster than the development of post-consumption saving on the part of consumers in every country. To accomplish this, however, businessmen will have to get away from thinking largely of export markets and be more concerned with their own domestic markets. The lack of interest on the part of too many businessmen and too many governments in domestic mass distribution is one of the real reasons why practically nothing has been done to encourage post-consumption saving. On the contrary, much has been done actually to discourage it.

Some years ago, when I was associated with Montgomery Ward and Company in Chicago, I made the revolutionary suggestion that we should sell everything on the installment plan, not just those things that could be repossessed. They had the old-fashioned idea then that unless something could be repossessed in case the customer didn't pay the bill, it should not be sold on the installment plan.

I pointed out that the repossession factor was a very unimportant element in the risk; the important thing was to insist that people pay their installment accounts on time. Later experience proved this to be true.

Two of the directors on the board who were conservative eastern bankers were very much against selling clothing, women's hosiery, men's wear, children's clothes, and such items on credit. Their chief argument was that they could not be repossessed and therefore they were a bad risk.

But I pointed out to them that we were selling paint on the installment plan, and obviously paint couldn't be scraped off the house to be repossessed either. This, fortunately, seemed to settle the argument, and we put everything in the catalogue on the installment plan. It took Sears, Roebuck almost two years before they followed us, so we zoomed ahead in business in a very spectacular way. In the latter of those two years, we did 82 per cent of Sears' volume. This has never been equaled since.

It's almost incredible to look back now and think how old-fashioned we all were in those days in our attitude about post-consumption saving. And the consumption of goods was far, far less in those days, too. Times, however, have certainly moved ahead, and now there is hardly anything that isn't sold on the installment plan, including vacation trips by sea and air, hotel accommodations, and practically everything else.

Perhaps some of this is going a bit too far, but one fact certainly stands out: without the enormous use of consumer credit today there wouldn't be the slightest possibility of absorbing the billions of dollars' worth of merchandise that flow through our distributive channels in this country every year.

CHAPTER

11

SERVICES

The tenth principle of distribution is *consumer services,* a subject well illustrated by this little incident.

One day last summer I was driving along a country road in Massachusetts when something went wrong with my motor. It began to knock rather loudly, and I became a bit alarmed. After a mile or so with the motor making a considerable racket, I came to a small town and drew up to a garage. One of the garagemen raised the hood, looked at the engine, and seemed to know what was wrong. He was a man of very few words, which is not unusual in rural Massachusetts. He simply pushed his cap back on his head, scratched his forehead, and walked into a stockroom.

After rummaging around for a while, he came out with something that I didn't recognize, since I am not familiar with automobile engines, hardly knowing a flywheel from a carburetor. Fortunately, this did not seem to be the case with the garageman. He very quickly and skillfully tinkered around, took out a part, inserted the new one in its place, and asked me to start the motor. Everything seemed to be sound as a bell again. I paid him and off I went.

Now, I tell this story to make the point that this same kind of service is available to any motorist in any state of the Union. If there is something wrong with his car, he can, within reason, drive into almost any service garage and have the matter repaired.

Not only can a consumer here buy one of the six million automobiles the manufacturers turn out and distribute through their enormous dealer organizations, but, what is equally important, he can have it repaired by skilled mechanics in almost every hamlet in the country.

Not only can skilled mechanics be found in most of these small places, but the *parts* are available as well. And this is very important, because a skillful and knowledgeable mechanic who hasn't got the parts at hand can do you very little good.

An efficient system of distribution cannot simply make available the original product, be it an automobile, a refrigerator, an electrical appliance, a tire, or any one of thousands of different items. To keep all these things in repair, a distribution system must have the repair parts stocked in various places all over the country and in the hands of skilled mechanics and repairmen who can use them for the consumer's benefit.

To make my point a little clearer, let me illustrate it this way. Not long ago it was announced that an American automobile dealer had gotten the franchise to distribute a Russian car. It is a car manufactured in not too large quantities in Russia and looks somewhat like a Dodge of approximately fifteen years ago. This man made a deal with the Soviets to obtain cars to be distributed throughout the United States.

In my opinion this venture is a doubtful one because there may not be enough spare parts quickly available in case of breakdown or trouble. The purchaser who buys one of these cars is taking the chance of finding it useless one fine day simply because something has gone wrong and it cannot be fixed.

That's why it took foreign cars so long to become established in this country. Dealers had to learn the trick of having spare parts properly distributed so they could be easily available in case of trouble. You cannot sell merchandise unless spare parts are readily at hand so repairs can be made in case of breakdowns. It is the system of distributing these parts all over the United States that undergirds the entire automobile, electrical-appliance, and similar mechanical industries.

The International Harvester Company is a good illustration of this. Not only do they sell their farmer customers reapers, combines, cotton pickers, and all sorts of farm machinery, but they have depots all over the farm country where they carry enormous stocks of spare parts to service all these machines. When a farmer is using his machine, he is generally in a hurry. He may be trying to gather in his grain ahead of possible rainy weather, and if his tractor or combine or reaper should break down, he is in a peck of trouble.

He has learned over the years that he can depend upon such companies as the International Harvester Company to come to his rescue immediately with the spare part he needs to make quick repairs. And this is the chief reason why this efficient corporation sells so much farm machinery. Farmers know they can depend on it in case of trouble.

There is a great deal of farm machinery that has to be kept in good working order in this country nowadays. For example, there are 12,500,000 farm cars, trucks, and tractors on the nation's farms today. It is estimated that the investment by farmers in machinery is twice that of the entire steel industry and five times that of the automobile industry. The average farm represents an investment in machinery of about $20,000 per worker. This is nearly $4,000 a worker more than in industry. So it is easy to see that not only is farming big business in America today, but a great deal of servicing is necessary to keep this enormous investment in machinery in repair and in good running order.

There was a piece in the newspapers awhile ago that had to do with the Soviet agricultural plan in Azerbaijan, one of Nikita Khrushchev's new projects designed to grow farm produce in an area that had been largely uninhabited. The experiment had not worked out for various reasons, one of which was that the farm machinery could not be repaired when it broke down.

Not only were skilled mechanics not available because the Russians have very few such people, but the spare parts were absolutely impossible to obtain. Consequently, when Khrushchev went down to inspect the area to see what the trouble was, he saw tractors, combines, and other farm machines standing immobile out in the fields. These had simply broken down, and because the spare parts were not obtainable had been left out in the fields to rust.

The real reason for the trouble is that the Russians seem to labor under the delusion that they need only make the original machines and that spare parts for repairs are not so important. This is because they have no real understanding of the function of distribution or the factors that are necessary to make distribution work. While they do distribute farm machinery, even though much of it is poorly made and therefore breaks down, they have no conception of the necessity for having spare parts stocked in handy places where they can be gotten at when repairs are needed.

Mr. Khrushchev, of course, blamed the fiasco on the prime minister of the area who, incidentally, had been one of his cronies personally appointed by him. Khrushchev said the minister should have called for help so he could have come to his rescue with a grandiose gesture. All of this was, of course, political double talk because what actually caused the fiasco was Khrushchev's ignorance of distribution. He just doesn't understand its first principles.

We in this country are so used to having spare parts and services readily available that we rarely give it a second thought. As a matter of fact, my little experience on the Massachusetts country road normally wouldn't have been thought of twice by the average American motorist. I suppose I did so only because of my deep interest in the subject of distribution.

But a moment's thought leads to the obvious conclusion that millions of automobiles, washing machines, radios, television sets, even electric toasters could not be distributed in such quantities if the customer had the slightest doubt about getting the repair services plus the spare parts necessary to keep them running. They must perform as millions of dollars' worth of advertising promised. The public is so aware of this that if it doesn't find these services in its immediate neighborhood, it gets very irate. Most business corporations are familiar with angry letters from customers when they discover their equipment cannot be properly serviced or the spare parts aren't available in the twinkling of an eye.

Last summer I had a rather interesting experience while trying to find a spare part for a lawn mower made many years ago and which had been discontinued. First I tried the local lawn-mower repairman. Then I drove a hundred miles to Springfield, Massachusetts, and tried the repairman there with no success. I went on to Hartford, Connecticut, and later to Pittsfield, Massachusetts, also without success.

I wasn't irritated by this because the lawn mower was so old that I really didn't expect to find anything. But I was most pleased with the thoughtful and courteous attention I received in most of these places. They tried to help me. But I finally had to have the spare part made by hand at rather considerable expense. I did this only because my gardener was so fond of the lawn mower that he just wouldn't have been happy with a new one.

Most people in America would much rather have bought a new one than repair the old one because they like to get the latest models. But my gardener happens to be a Frenchman who gets attached to things and he wanted to keep his old lawn mower because he is used to it. Incidentally, my excursions around the countryside were an eye opener. I was amazed to find so many service places for lawn mowers. There is no other country in the world where you can find such convenient consumer services and so generally staffed by efficient and skilled mechanics as in America. This is a very real and vital cornerstone in the distribution structure.

THE ELEMENT OF
MASS TRANSPORTATION

The eleventh foundation stone upon which mass distribution rests is *mass transportation.*

If we didn't have the facilities for transporting the huge quantities that are produced each year quickly and speedily, it is, of course, quite obvious that mass distribution would not work.

There are several systems of transportation that play an important part in moving goods from producer to consumer and one of the oldest, of course, is the railroad. Although rail transportation has become less important as the years have gone on, it still is a major factor. Not only do the railroads move coal, fuel, etc., to the points of consumption, but the finished merchandise is very often moved by rail to the points of final distribution. Then, of course, the railroad systems transport large numbers of salesmen who travel around the country calling on wholesalers, retailers, etc., selling merchandise and services.

In some backward countries such as Soviet Russia, China, and other parts of Asia and Africa, railroads are rather few and far between and, consequently, very overloaded and crowded. Most of the transportation in those countries has been along the great rivers which have been the highways for cheap transportation for many hundreds and sometimes thousands of years. Our rivers in the United States, of course, are also important, but they play a relatively minor role because of the other facilities available. It is no longer possible to depend too much on river transportation in the modern world. It is a factor, but not one of major importance any more for obvious reasons.

In this connection we should also mention the great ocean-going steamship services that carry all the import and export trade between the continents of the world. There is no need to go into it in any great detail, but the importance of ocean traffic is obviously enormous.

The most rapidly growing and probably the most important facility today for transporting goods is the truck. It has an advantage over the railroad because it is very often able to transport goods from one point to another with only one handling. Merchandise can be picked up at the point of origin and trucked right through to the point of destination without having to be unloaded from the truck. If you ship by rail, you must first truck the merchandise to the railroad station; then it has to be picked up at the other end by truck again. This makes for at least three handling, which sometimes causes breakage and damage.

The extent of the truck service in the United States is enormous. There are more than 11,000,000 trucks operating at the present time and the number is growing steadily. This compares to 1,777,000 freight cars in use in the United States. So it's easy to see how important truck transportation has become. Of course much merchandise is hauled in smaller vehicles, private cars, etc., especially to nearby points. There are more than 81,000,000 people in the United States who have drivers' licenses, including truck and bus licenses, so there are plenty of people to carry the goods produced by our factories into the channels of distribution.

The fourth factor, of course, has to do with an adequate network of roads which is necessary if any efficient automobile transportation is to exist. This has been highly developed in the United States and is being improved constantly with enormous grants of money from the federal government and the states so we may have a satisfactory road and highway system.

There is very little doubt that if we didn't have our highly developed road system we would not have advanced in mass distribution to the present level.

The interrelationship of all these factors is very important. One cannot exist without the other. It just wouldn't be possible to have all the great store and factory facilities that we have in the United States if we didn't have the roads over which food and other merchandise could be shipped to these hundreds of thousands of chain and department stores as well as factories. It enables the public in every small American town to find good merchandise and good food products at reasonable prices. Therefore, any country that is anxious to build up its mass distribution must have a network of good roads and the trucks necessary to move the goods.

Countries in the Soviet bloc are very handicapped by the fact that they have very few roads, many of which are bad. This means that they have to move almost all their merchandise by rail, which isn't adequate enough to handle the situation because they are also lacking in rail facilities.

An interesting example of this came to light at last February's meeting in Moscow of the eastern European ministers. The Soviet government informed them that they would no longer be able to ship iron ore to the great steel mills that had been built during the last ten years in Poland, Rumania, East Germany, Hungary, and Bulgaria. This was a great blow because these mills are totally dependent on this Soviet ore. And what was the reason? It was too much of a burden on the Russian transportation system, said the Soviets.

So building factories in these places just isn't enough. If they don't develop good roads so the products can be efficiently moved to the points of distribution, the factories will have to limit their production to the transportation facilities available.

Any schoolboy understands that the amount of water you can force through a one-inch pipe is limited by the size of the pipe. No matter how much pressure you apply, the amount will not vary very much. If you want more water, you increase the gauge of the pipe. The same principle holds with transportation. Limited facilities will handle limited amounts of goods. To achieve mass distribution you must have mass transportation.

The fifth important transportation facility is the airplane. More and more cargo planes are flying on routes all over this country, and people who have to ship things that must arrive quickly are making greater and greater use of them. This form of transportation has grown enormously. In 1959 the air lines transported 595,000,-000 ton-miles of freight in America, or as much every nine days as they carried in the entire year of 1946. Thirty-eight times as many ton-miles of freight were moved in 1959 as in 1946.

Air cargo has other advantages over other forms of transportation. Where shipment by rail or truck requires expensive protective packing, shipment by air often does not. The International Business Machines Corporation has found that it can now ship electronic computers by air merely wrapped in brown paper. A well-known motorcycle manufacturer ships his product completely assembled and factory-adjusted by air at a net saving of $7.50 per machine by eliminating reassembly and adjustment at destination. They simply strap the motorcycle to a dolly and put it on the plane.

Until recently aircraft engines were shipped by surface transportation in heavy metal containers that had to be returned. Now these engines are being flown to the West Coast packaged only in zippered plastic bags and bolted to shipping stands. The Boeing Company has estimated that for the first one hundred 707's which it produced, shipping the four hundred engines by air in the manner described above resulted in a saving on shipping costs of more than $750,000.

Bonwit Teller uses the air lines frequently. Ready-to-wear merchandise is sent from New York to its branches in Chicago, Cleveland, and Palm Beach by air because there are often advertising deadlines to meet, and the merchandise must be there when the ads run in the newspapers. It is, of course, a little more expensive than truck or rail transportation, but if the unit value of the merchandise is high enough and the weight low enough, it can be very economical because of the time saved.

This is something that I feel offers great opportunities to backward countries that haven't got good roads or adequate rail transportation. They can fly merchandise over rough terrain much more inexpensively and save the capital required to build a network of highways. It seems to me that this will be the general transportation of the future in countries such as India where the distances are enormous and where not enough capital will be available to build the roads necessary to support growing mass distribution.

It seems to me that old airplanes, that is, propeller-driven ones, rather than expensive jets, can be utilized for this type of transportation. As the older planes are made obsolete by jets in the more highly developed and industrialized countries, it seems to me they can be sold secondhand to more backward countries for freight transportation. In any case, I should think that standardized cargo-carrying planes could be manufactured in quantity at more reasonable prices for this kind of work than the enormously expensive super jets that are now being built for passenger travel.

A sixth method of mass transportation is the pipeline. This, of course, is largely used to transport oil from oil wells to points of consumption as well as other liquid or gaseous products of various kinds. The use of pipelines is also growing and is particularly helpful in places such as our Midwest or other flat places. In desert areas, too, like the Sahara, where it is impractical to build highways or to fly such products by air, the pipeline is extremely useful. It is a rather new factor but a rapidly growing one.

The seventh element in the transportation picture is the private automobile.

Sixty million automobiles running around our highways play an enormous role in mass transportation. They not only enable consumers to come in to shopping areas where they can buy merchandise and take it with them to their homes, but they also transport many people to their places of work in cities as well as along highways.

This private transportation has enabled many factories to buy farm land just off good highways and build factories all on one floor, with plenty of parking space for their employees. Here they don't have to worry about being next to a railroad siding which used to be the requirement years ago, because now products are shipped by truck.

The fact that the consumer is so mobile in the United States makes for very keen competition. Not only can he go from door to door on Main Street to see where he can buy what he wants most advantageously, but he and his wife can just hop in the car and drive off to the next village to see what they can get there. This sometimes makes for a lot of cutthroat competition, but it certainly insures the consumer against being overcharged.

Such transportation is just not possible in many countries around the world because they lack auto facilities. But as cars become increasingly available, those merchants who have banded together in a little town to keep their prices up will find that the merchants in the next town are underselling them and they must meet that competition. This, of course, will be good for the consumer, but it is so different from the way most merchants run their businesses in foreign countries that it will come as quite a shock.

The greatest transportation handicap in this country is the lack of parking space. Most of our cities grew up during the era when there were no automobiles or very few of them, and the streets are all too narrow for the proper handling of traffic. No parking facilities were even thought necessary. Consequently, almost every town and big city in the United States is beset by the traffic and parking problem.

If this problem had been dealt with twenty-five years ago, we would be very much better off now, and I believe our volume of business would be much greater than it is today. Today business is handicapped by this lack of parking space.

For years the administration of the city of New York discouraged the building of parking garages. They made the person who wanted to build one go through the most complicated procedure to get a permit to build. If you wished to buy a piece of land and build a parking garage on it, you had to gamble on getting your permit through the Board of Aldermen (now the Board of Estimate). If they refused your application, you had your money tied up in a piece of real estate that was generally not good for anything else.

There was undoubtedly some graft connected with this cumbersome procedure, but the net result was that very few parking garages, certainly not enough to meet the need, were ever built in the city of New York. Today the city fathers are trying to encourage the building of parking garages, but now, of course, the price of land has gone so high that it is very difficult to make them a paying investment.

As a consequence, most New Yorkers simply park their cars on the street, and because of the large number of cars involved, the city authorities are reluctant to enforce the anti-parking regulations. The cars just sit there and make it impossible for traffic to get through the streets. Very often cars are even double-parked on both sides of the street so that you have to go through single file and it takes much too long to get any place.

Downtown shopping areas are losing out and a great

number of suburban shopping centers are springing up all over the country. Since these shopping centers are being built during an era when everyone is thinking about parking, they have very adequate and convenient parking areas for their customers. This makes it much more desirable for the average suburban customer to drive in to a shopping center to do his shopping than to come into town.

The downtown situation, however, is becoming more and more serious because of our inability to cope with the parking problem. Heroic efforts will have to be made by city governments and groups of businessmen to bring some real improvement to this situation. If real improvement doesn't come soon, a great deal of money will be lost in blighted downtown shopping areas that represent billions of dollars of investment, not to mention the business lost through the decreased distribution of goods.

In most cities in Europe the situation is even more unsatisfactory, because most of these towns and cities were built several hundred years ago when no one dreamed of an automobile, and when in many instances the streets were deliberately made narrow because the chief concern was defense against marauding bandits or enemy troops. Consequently, the parking facilities abroad will become worse and worse as more automobiles come into general use. They have tried to solve the problem by making smaller automobiles, which helps to some extent, but the parking situation abroad will become increasingly bad.

The parking problem is a serious deterrent to mass

distribution. Much money will have to be invested in parking facilities before it can be substantially improved. Many cities are trying to meet the problem by building parking facilities under parks. The city of Chicago has one that parks 2,000 cars under one of its water-front parks, and the city of Newark is now in the process of building one under the square right in the middle of the city. Boston is also building a parking area under Boston Common. But much more needs to be done. We are more backward in furnishing parking facilities than in anything else that affects distribution, and much future capital will have to be invested to solve it.

Perhaps traffic in and out of our large cities may be improved eventually by the wider use of the helicopter. The one place where we still have some space in our overcrowded cities is on our rooftops, and it seems to me that if we could furnish people with helicopter service from vast parking lots in the suburbs this might be one way of solving the problem. By charging higher toll rates at our bridges and thus forcing people to park in designated areas in the suburbs, we could transport them by giant helicopters into certain central areas in the city.

During the last war there was a helicopter service from the airport in Boston to the roof of the Statler Hotel. The trip took only six minutes, whereas by taxi through the Sumner Tunnel it was a forty-five-minute trip. I personally used it frequently because the Bonwit store in Boston was just two short blocks away from the Statler Hotel. Perhaps in the future we will be able to build helicopters that carry larger loads and are not so noisy so we can utilize this new approach to urban transportation more widely.

Something needs to be done about this. Otherwise billions of dollars of investments will be lost because of the parking and traffic problems in and out of our large cities.

13

SALESMANSHIP

One of the foundation stones and the twelfth principle upon which distribution is built is *salesmanship*.

All the way through the process, as well as in the final stages of distribution, the force that moves merchandise is salesmanship. Although this seems to be an elementary idea, it is amazing how little of it is actually practiced.

For example, take the situation on the Island of Murano just outside of Venice where Venetian glass has been made since the ninth century. In the early days the workers were kept as prisoners on the island, not allowed to leave under any circumstances. This was done because they didn't want to share their secret of glass-making with anyone else. The people who now make the glass on Murano are mainly the descendants of these ancient glassblowers, and the island is studded with small partnerships, companies, and groups of workmen who make this well-known Venetian glass.

When you step out of your gondola or, if you wish, your motorboat, you go into their showrooms, some of which are rather well done and up to date. But there is no such thing as a salesman. The person who comes out to greet you is generally one of the bookkeepers or an accountant, or occasionally the factory manager. The proverbial needle in the haystack is easier to find than a salesman on the Island of Murano.

So what do you do? Well, you simply buy. No one tries to sell you anything. You have to ask questions: can they do it this way, or can they do it that way; if you buy a larger quantity, can you get a better price; can you change the colors; can you have it exclusively for your particular store, etc., etc.?

You wander around the showroom and pick up things, look at them, trying to use your imagination on how you can adapt them to your particular purpose. But the bookkeeper who is taking care of you never offers any suggestion of any kind.

The Island of Murano is not an extreme case. I cite it as a good example of the age-old method of producing merchandise and letting the process stop there. Not the slightest bit of effort, skill, or planning is made to sell it. There is no advertising and absolutely no salesman-ship. They tell you what they can do and what they can't do, how much it costs, when they can deliver, and that's all. This lack of salesmanship holds in a great many places in Europe and in the rest of the world as well.

For centuries the accepted method of selling at wholesale in Europe was through the trade fair. It reached its highest development in Germany in the old days with the Leipzig Fair. Since the conquest of East Germany by the Russians, the Leipzig Fair has not been what it used to be.

But West Germany developed its own fair in the city of Hanover. This Hanover Fair is really magnificent. Anyone who hasn't seen it finds it difficult to imagine. Most people think of fairs as consumer fairs, like the Brussels Fair or the World's Fair in New York, Chicago, etc. The Hanover Fair, however, is a fair that sells at wholesale and does it very well.

This magnificent fair is a once-a-year proposition, and it runs for only about two weeks. It covers several square miles, and there are acres and acres of permanent buildings housing great quantities of merchandise. It parks about twenty thousand automobiles and draws about a million and a half people to the small city of Hanover.

There is an entire building about the size of Madison Square Garden that houses nothing but electric dynamos. There is another building, with nothing but porcelains, silverware, and jewelry, which has six floors completely equipped with escalators. There are also buildings for machine tools, for leather goods, and acres and acres of buildings for almost everything they make in Germany.

Professional buyers who are interested in the German

market go to the Hanover Fair. They go to these permanently established showrooms to do their buying. The Germans, of course, know a good deal more about selling than the Venetians on the Island of Murano, and you are generally well taken care of. A real effort is made to sell you the merchandise.

However, in my opinion, trade fairs are not enough to move the quantities of merchandise necessary to improve the level of prosperity. Our method, on the wholesale level, is not only to maintain showrooms in central cities, but to put our salesmen on the road to call on the trade.

This, of course, has become much more highly developed through the use of automobile transportation and the airplane because the salesman can travel around to see his customers more conveniently than he could when he was dependent upon railroad transportation alone.

Nowhere in the world has the art of selling at wholesale been developed to as high a point as it has in the United States. Sales programs, sales conventions, and sales meetings are planned and carried out by highly skilled sales executives. There is hardly a company in this country that doesn't dignify this activity by heading it with a corporate officer, such as a vice-president, or often an executive vice-president, because it realizes how important the sales function is. No one in America believes the old adage that if you "build a better mousetrap, the world will beat a path to your door." We found out long ago that this idea is as dead as the dodo. To achieve the mass distribution we must have, our sales executives must beat the path to the door of the *customer* instead of the other way around. That is why we have developed the art of salesmanship on the wholesale level to the point it has reached. And that is why our distribution is far ahead of the rest of the world.

When you reach the retail level, you find Europe much more skilled at it than at wholesale selling. As a matter of fact, it's pretty hard to get out of a store without buying in Europe because the salesmanship is very good and of a high order. It is at least as good as it is in the United States, and often better. The European seems more interested in the customer than his or her counterpart in the United States. He is generally more courteous and agreeable.

What is salesmanship? Let's examine it in more detail and perhaps we can arrive at a better understanding of what it is.

My definition of salesmanship is this. It is the art of *leading a customer to a decision.* Now, what does that mean?

Well, first of all, let us discuss what it should not mean. Most people react badly to what they call high-pressure salesmanship. By that they mean the salesman who tries to push merchandise they really don't want down their throats, and who uses strong and forceful methods to try to get them to buy. This has been the target of much criticism of late years and is often called the "hard sell."

The trouble with this approach is that the salesman is trying to get the customer to do what he, the salesman, wants him to do rather than trying to get the customer to do what the customer herself or himself really would like to do. And that, of course, is not the essence of good salesmanship.

The first principle of salesmanship is that the salesman be sincerely *interested* in the customer. He should try to find out the customer's need and then find exactly the right kind of merchandise to fit that particular customer's need.

Of course, not every customer knows exactly what she wants when she steps into a store. Sometimes she has a very vague idea what she is looking for. It takes a very skilled salesman to crystallize the customer's own ideas so they can finally be focused on something that the customer feels is exactly what she wants.

This is what I mean by "leading" the customer to a decision. The salesman must never, under any circumstances, make the customer feel that she is being "forced" to a decision. That gets back again to high-pressure selling. He must convince the customer through good salesmanship that she is arriving at her own decision. He does this by focusing her attention more and more firmly on something that seems to satisfy her need. And when that point is reached, the skilled salesman or saleswoman helps the customer make the final decision to buy.

Of course, the crucial point is the making of this decision by the customer. If there is anything that most people hate to do, it is to make a decision. Coming to a decision requires mental energy and real thought, and most people have a very difficult time doing it even when the result doesn't cost them any money.

But when one is buying merchandise, the decision always costs money, and this makes the average person even more reluctant to decide. At this point the skilled salesman knows how to help the customer make the decision and also makes the customer feel this is just what she wants to do.

A very important element in salesmanship is, of course, *knowledge of the product*. The salesman must have real knowledge about what he is selling. It takes a lot of effort on the part of the salesman to learn all about his product: how the product is made, how good the materials are, and how the product will perform. This is not too difficult to learn if the salesman is selling a fairly limited number of products. For example, if he is a salesman in an automobile showroom, he needs to know about five or six models. But if the salesman is in a department store, he must know about a great many, sometimes hundreds, of products. While this is a very difficult thing to do, the salesman who doesn't know his product or products is obviously at a disadvantage.

Next, the salesman must understand the product's *benefit points*. Now a benefit point is what the product will *do* for the consumer. This is even more important than knowledge of the product itself, because in the final analysis the consumer buys something because it benefits *her,* and not because it is made of this, that, or the other thing.

For example, she isn't the slightest bit interested in the quality of the steel in her refrigerator. She probably couldn't care less, but she *is* interested in what the refrigerator will do for her. And if the salesman can point out that the quality of the metal in the refrigerator is superior in a way that will guarantee her more benefits than one made of some other alloy, that is of importance to the customer. It means it is going to do something that benefits her.

At this point the element of imagination enters the sales process. Imagination is something that distinguishes salesmanship from many other pursuits. A salesman cannot function without imagination. There may be lots of other occupations that can, but not salesmanship.

I remember sitting next to a savings-bank president one time at a charity dinner. I asked him what quality he felt was most necessary for success in the savings-bank business. He thought for a long time, and then said, "Well, I don't know what quality is most needed, but I can tell you what quality you shouldn't have under any circumstances."

I asked, "What is that?"

He said, "Imagination."

We both laughed, but then he explained that if a person has too much imagination, he might easily get the bank into some wildcat scheme that would not be good for the depositors.

But in salesmanship, imagination is a prime requisite. Unless the salesman has the imagination to see what a product can do for the customer and then the ability to point these things out, it will not be possible for him to lead that customer to the decision to buy.

A salesman must also be genuinely interested in people. He must be friendly and have a pleasant and engaging personality. It may be all right for a statistician or a bookkeeper to be dour and cold with people so long as he can figure rapidly, but a salesman obviously will not be very successful unless he first of all can "sell" himself to the customer as a person that the customer would like to deal with.

I know many successful saleswomen who make such fast friends of their customers that they often receive presents and letters, and sometimes their customers just drop in to have a little social chat with them.

Some years ago I read a letter from a prominent Englishwoman who had bought some clothes from a saleswoman at Bonwit Teller to go to the durbar in India. She wrote the most charming letter, telling the sales clerk how she looked in her beautiful evening clothes at the great ball given by the Viceroy.

One superb saleswoman of my acquaintance once took an automobile trip with her husband to New England during one of her vacations. Before she left, she made a list of the addresses of the country residences of her customers who lived in that area. She stopped and made notes about their houses, hedges, lawns, etc. When her customers came in that fall she would look up her notes and remark about their houses or lawns, much to their obvious delight. This is supersalesmanship in the finest sense.

A good salesperson very often advises a customer *against* buying merchandise. She does this if she sincerely feels that it is not suitable, because she is wise enough to know that if the customer begins to feel that the salesperson's advice is in her interest, then the customer-salesman relationship reaches a really high point of confidence.

This is very much like a doctor-patient relationship that exists basically on the confidence between the patient and the doctor. The salesman-customer relationship should be exactly the same. The customer should feel that she can rely absolutely on the salesman's advice and that the salesman is by no means primarily interested in just pushing more and more merchandise at her.

It doesn't take much insight, it seems to me, to realize the important role that salesmanship plays in the distribution of vast quantities of merchandise. Nevertheless, there are a great many people all over the world who don't realize how important it is.

What do we find in Russia? I am told there is an almost total absence of salesmanship. But of course with the present scarcity of merchandise salesmanship is hardly necessary. There is a feeling that it never will be, a belief which will bring them a rude jolt someday.

People in Russia simply stand in line for food, clothing, and other necessities. When they arrive at the counter in the government-run department stores, such as GUM in Moscow, they are treated with the utmost contempt by their comrade saleswomen. Not the slightest interest on the part of the clerk is in evidence. As a matter of fact, the clerk doesn't even remotely resemble a saleswoman. She is just a person who hands out the merchandise and sends the customers to stand in another line where they pay their money.

If the standard of living is going to rise and finally equal ours in the United States, as Mr. Khrushchev is telling everyone it will, the element of salesmanship will have to be developed in Russia. People just aren't going to stand in line and buy merchandise except when they are on the barest subsistence level.

But salesmanship cannot function under communism. Salesmanship requires a free spirit which cannot function under government supervision. Even in our own country, we can see examples of why salesmanship cannot function under government enterprise. How often have you gotten a smile from a government clerk? No, salesmanship is simply not possible except under privately owned and privately operated free enterprise.

If Karl Marx had had any understanding of the role that salesmanship plays in the distribution of goods, he would never have written his Manifesto. He merely thought in terms of production. Distribution to him was a very vague thing. Nowhere in his writings is there a hint that he understood anything about distribution.

Russia, of course, also lacks the store facilities that are so familiar in the West. There are few independent shopkeepers, no chain stores, except for a few government-run ones. And, in my opinion, there never will be any under their system of state-run capitalism.

You may be able to build and run factories under communism, but there is one thing you cannot do, and that is complete the final stages of distribution through large, medium, and small stores. There can be no vast network of stores under any other system except the private property, free-enterprise system.

Not only is this type of activity forbidden under communism, but if the Kremlin should ever liberalize communism enough to introduce such a network of stores, they would not succeed because you cannot run stores under government restrictions. At least you cannot run stores that do any great volume of business. If Mr. Khrushchev had any idea or any understanding of mass distribution, he, of course, would see this. But he thinks totally in terms of production. When he brags that he is going to improve the standard of living in Russia and catch up with the United States, he had better learn something about distribution.

Salesmanship is that magic catalyst that finally makes the customer (be he a wholesale or a retail customer) make that fateful decision to pay out his money for the product. This one act, multiplied hundreds of millions of times, is what makes the whole economic machine function.

However, in my opinion, we in the West have also neglected the training of salesmanship. Good salesmen and good saleswomen are getting harder and harder to obtain. I don't know what will happen to the distribution system if some real effort is not made to try to develop more salesmen.

There are universities that teach business administration, marketing, economics, engineering, architecture, accounting, and almost every skill necessary for the operation of vast business enterprises. But you hardly ever run across a course on salesmanship in any of these universities.

What good are all these other skills if in the final analysis no one can convince the customer to buy? Since all their jobs actually depend upon him, it's simply amazing how little effort is expended to teach salesmanship.

Some people feel that salesmanship can't be taught, that a salesman is born. I don't agree. You cannot make a salesman out of a bookkeeper or an engineer out of an actor; but you can take normally intelligent, outgoing, pleasant people and teach them enough about salesmanship so they can be extremely effective.

I think courses should be given in grammar schools, high schools, colleges, and business schools on salesmanship. If nothing else comes out of this activity, at least some people would be taught how to be polite, how to be thoughtful, how to think a little about others instead of thinking only about themselves. One of the prime requirements of a salesman is the ability to think about the other person's wants and needs and forget about himself.

Because of the scarcity of salesmen, chain stores have tended to turn more and more to "self-service." People have gotten used to picking the packages off the racks themselves. This is of course a wonderful way to sell certain types of merchandise. But even this merchandise can't be sold without preconditioning the customer through advertising, which is just a form of salesmanship.

Advertising, after all, is nothing more than "salesmanship in print." The customers in the grocery store have been exposed to millions of dollars' worth of "salesmanship in print" to which they react as they wheel their little buggies up and down the aisles. If you stopped this "salesmanship in print," you would find that such self-service stores would lose a very large percentage of their business. So salesmanship even in self-service stores is of vital importance.

When you get into quality merchandise, and merchandise that is a little higher in price, then good personal salesmanship is absolutely necessary. This merchandise just does not sell itself. It requires a very skilled, expert, knowledgeable, interested, and enthusiastic salesperson to help the customer come to a decision.

And let me emphasize the word "enthusiastic." There can be no salesmanship without enthusiasm. There are lots of other occupations that can function fairly well without enthusiasm, but not salesmanship. One reason selling is so difficult for some people is that it is not easy to maintain a high level of enthusiasm.

I talked the other day with a national advertiser who spends more than twenty million dollars a year advertising his products. He had recently made an anonymous tour visiting stores to test the salesmanship on his products. He was simply appalled at the service he got and at the lack of enthusiasm on the part of the salespeople.

He said to me, "Why should I spend millions of dollars a year to advertise my product when it is all ruined by the unenthusiastic, stupid, and negligent service that is given to the customer as she tries to buy it?"

Not only do national advertisers spend millions of dollars advertising their products, but most of them spend more millions to send demonstrators around the country whose job it is to train the salesmen at the point of sale. But these demonstrators are hardly in a position to teach much beyond the bare esentials about their products. They cannot instill into the salesclerks the elements of courtesy, interest, enthusiasm, or the imagination necessary to sell effectively. The great store organizations, of course, spend millions of dollars training their salespeople, but sometimes their efforts seem to be poorly rewarded.

I have tried to demonstrate what an important keystone salesmanship is in the distribution arch. We need to give the subject much more serious thought and expend much more energy and money to teach it.

If we expect our economy to grow, we should give a great deal more attention to salesmanship. It is one of the most important elements in mass distribution.

14

PROFESSIONALISM

The thirteenth principle of mass distribution is *professionalism*.

More professionalism is needed in all phases of distribution than we have at the present time. Great strides have been made in America, but not in very many other places.

Since the days when the Phoenicians plied the Mediterranean in their open ships, most phases of distribution have not measured up to the professionalism in other occupations.

Even as long as 4,000 years ago the Pyramids in Egypt

were built by professionals who were quite obviously knowledgeable in geometry and engineering. As a matter of fact, this engineering job was even more remarkable than some of the engineering feats we perform today because people then lacked the tools and machinery that are available now.

But it is only lately, and principally in America, that we have become conscious of the need for professionalism in distribution. We need more graduate as well as undergraduate courses in distribution, and we need to give degrees in advertising, transportation, retailing, selling, designing, display, etc.

As a matter of fact, designing is one of the few fields that has become professionalized, and many schools of design have been established. But we have only scratched the surface here and we need to establish many, many more. When one considers the fact that hardly a thing is produced today that does not depend on some type of designing, you can see the enormous importance of this one phase of distribution. More attention, too, needs to be paid from a professional standpoint to styling. Too much of it today is purely hit and miss and on a very amateur level.

Then, of course, the study of fashion in all its facets is something that is carried on today on a very nonprofessional level. We need to have more information about fashion cycles. We need measurements of their duration, how they start, what makes them stop, and why they are embraced by the general public.

If you must have a professional architect to design a building and a professional engineer to build it, it seems to me just as necessary to have professionals in designing, styling, and fashion if we are to do a better job in these fields in the future.

I was talking to the vice president in charge of styling of one of the large automobile companies recently and here are some of the interesting facts he told me. He directs a staff of 1,275 people who are housed in a modern, glass-walled studio building. They have every facility at their beck and call to do their styling job. He has designers, stylists, colorists, engineers, clay modelers, draftsmen, and model makers by the score.

In designing one of their automobiles, the stylist first creates theme sketches. These sketches are followed by full-sized drawings. After these drawings have been scrutinized, clay models and trim bucks are built. Trim bucks are models of interiors corresponding to the clay models of the exteriors.

Once approval of these has been given, a plastic model is built and painted. It has chrome parts, glass windshield, rear window, side windows, and everything.

This styling chief and his staff must anticipate the varying moods, attitudes, and needs of a changable public and attempt to provide it with all kinds of specialized vehicles in the years ahead.

The major influences on such designs, of course, will be the way the present models sell, the public reaction to the experimental "dream cars," new engineering developments, the changing living and working habits of the American populace, and, finally, and by no means least important, how women react to the models.

It wasn't too many years ago that the feminine influence was largely a stern voice from the back seat, suggesting that Dad slow down. Today the woman has moved to the front seat, drives the car half the time and, in many cases of course, has one of her own.

The fashion trend at the present time, according to this style authority, is toward quieter colors and less chrome on the exterior. He says they have to put interest and character into their cars because styling is what really sells them. If a person doesn't like the styling of a car, he won't walk through an open door to look at it even though it has the best of engineering.

Here you have an example of a professional approach to styling in this one industry. The same approach is needed in many others. Of course, all companies are not able to have such large styling and designing staffs, but professional designing firms, of which there are several, can offer this kind of service at a moderate cost.

Even this service is in its infancy, and, consequently, too many manufacturers depend upon copying and adapting what they find other people doing. This makes for sameness, lacks imagination, and in the long run is self-defeating.

Consequently, there is a great need for people in distribution who have had a broad cultural background. You cannot have taste or be a judge of design unless you have had the advantage of a liberal-arts education which has been rather heavily weighted in the direction of fine arts and design.

It is possible, of course, to acquire such a background and many people have done so. But what is required is not amateur, but professional, taste that is based upon a broad knowledge of art history and the study of design through the great design periods of the past.

Too many people in business today, when asked their opinions on such matters, merely say, "Yes, I like this" or "No, I don't like that." That, of course, is not a professional approach.

More and more companies whose business it is to sell good design are requiring that their executives be people who have such a broad cultural background. Many of these companies also have art experts on their staffs, particularly experts in the applied arts who can work with their designers and advise them on good design and good style.

This professional approach is the only proper way of tackling the problem, and as time goes on there will be an increasing demand for such people. The uncultured but aggressive man who was able to make a success in the old days will be at a disadvantage in the years to come when he competes with a team that includes people who have a professional knowledge of design based on a broad cultural education and background.

More professionalism is also required in the retail end of distribution. Too many jobs are currently performed by people who haven't much more than an amateur status. In time some of them may gain a more professional approach, but a great deal of money may be lost while they learn. Most of them have to be taught on the job, so to speak, because hardly any are available who have received formal training in any phases of retail operations. Now there are, of course, some schools in America which are doing work in retailing, but this is also a unique American development that doesn't exist at all in England, on the Continent, or in any other place in the world.

More and more foreign retailers are sending people over to study American methods of retail distribution because they realize how far ahead of most of them we are. Many countries in Asia, Africa, and the Soviet bloc, however, haven't arrived at the point where they even realize the need for such professionalism.

Everyone, of course, is familiar with the fact that the Soviet school system is heavily weighted to produce scientists and engineers, and I sometimes wonder what they're all going to do when their production programs run head on into their lack of distribution know-how. If the Soviet system hasn't cracked up for other reasons by that time, it certainly is going to receive a severe jolt, a jolt from which it may perhaps never recover. As a matter of fact, I think it is quite likely that when that happens, some of their wiser heads may begin to realize that state capitalism is basically an unworkable thing unless you keep your people on a bare subsistence level.

The evidence is beginning to accumulate that such trouble is already brewing in the Soviet Union. Stocks of merchandise are backing up and the Soviets are becoming concerned about it.

The official magazine of the State Planning Committee, the *Planovoye Khozyaistvo,* ran an article on it not so long ago. Here's what it had to say.

"Unwanted merchandise is piling up in warehouses and storerooms. Volume increases in consumer-goods production no longer result automatically in increased sales."

That's quite an admission. Perhaps the Soviet bureaucrats are beginning to sense that something is wrong. The magazine went on to say that "irresponsible distribution also accounts for stock piles of unwanted goods" and that "Leningrad early last year received three times as much drapery material as it had ordered but only half the clothing material it wanted, whereas the reverse occurred elsewhere." Warehouse stocks are increasing at an undesirable rate, the magazine added.

The article warned that costly surpluses of some goods would develop if production schedules were not matched to scientific studies of demand. It recommended "extensive and continuing studies of buying habits in place of the traditional gauging of demand by the amount of money in the pockets of Russian consumers."

After this article appeared, the government tried to correct the overstocking by cutting prices on some goods including jam, silk, and some radios, cameras and sewing machines. But the government planners said "major adjustments in production and distribution were needed to keep in step with consumer demand."

This is an interesting and revealing article, and, in my opinion, is a harbinger of more serious distribution problems in the near future for the Soviet Union. But more important, it indicates a glimmer of awareness that something is wrong with their distribution machinery and that a more professional approach will be required to solve it.

Lastly, let me say that we in America are much more conscious of the need for a professional approach in distribution than other countries. In most foreign countries, the best brains and the people with the best education tend to go into the professions and into production work. The people with the poorest educational backgrounds tend to end up in distribution.

In this country, however, all types of distribution work are on as high a level as any of the other occupations. We have many more people in distribution with college and professional degrees than can be found in any other country in the world. In my opinion, this is one of the reasons why we have developed so far beyond other countries in mass distribution.

CHAPTER

15

CONCLUSION

Let us try to take an objective look at some of the philosophy behind our great production and distribution system. I think it might be particularly helpful to foreign businessmen.

Our economic philosophy is quite different from the philosophy of other countries. Some of it, of course, is quite obvious and some of it is not. One of the differences is the relationship between management and employees. In many foreign countries, employees have inherited a rather menial position. We have gotten entirely away from any such feeling here.

CONCLUSION

I have gone through many factories in foreign countries, and it always struck me that the workers were generally silent and glum when the boss walked through. Hardly ever did he stop to chat with them. They seemed to be rather hostile and sometimes even resentful.

If you walk through an American factory with the factory manager, or through an American store or other business enterprise, you get quite a different impression. The boss is generally quite well acquainted with his workers. They seem to be on a more friendly basis. He stops and chats with them and is very often familiar with their personal and family problems. There seems to be no relationship of inferior and superior.

Perhaps this is because the European economic system evolved out of the feudal system and is still permeated with class distinctions. Here in America our economic system grew up with the free settlers. There were no inherited class distinctions and the feudal system had been left behind in Europe.

Consequently, the relationship is quite different and this, I think, is important. Management and labor here work together more harmoniously and much more sympathetically. At least they did up until the time of the depression when the union movement began to be led by people who in some instances retained certain influences from their European backgrounds. Some of these men were used to the feudal relationships that existed in Europe and tended to carry them over into their relationships here. They stressed the doctrine that there was a basic conflict between management and labor, that their interests were incompatible, and that essentially they were irreconcilable foes. This was the Old World concept. It had never been our idea in America of the relationship between management and labor.

Nobody questions that workers work for management. But the big difference between the American concept and the foreign concept is that here the managers of a business feel very deeply that they are also working for the workers. In other words, it's a two-way relationship. This is basically an American concept that foreign visitors find very puzzling.

The workers here feel that if the business is successful, they will also benefit. The American worker knows that American management understands the advantage to the enterprise of creating good working conditions, dealing fairly with them and, above all, paying good wages. The relationship has a mutuality that doesn't exist in many other places in the world.

Many foreign visitors like to dwell on the fact that the American businessman is interested only in making money. Of course he's interested in making money, but he is also in business because he finds the game fascinating, again an attitude that is quite different from that of his counterpart abroad. Consequently, he is able to impart his enthusiasm to his workers very much more successfully than is possible elsewhere.

In too many businesses abroad, the whole enterprise is run without much enthusiasm. It's just a job. It's just a way to make a living and there is no thrill to it, no fun in it. It is just a dull thing to get away from as soon as the bell rings.

Enthusiasm on the part of both the American worker

and American management is one of the key factors in making a cooperative relationship between management and labor. It has been a very important factor in developing mass production and mass distribution to such a high point. Most people in American business, be they workers or managers, like what they're doing. They're having fun doing it. They enjoy beating their former records, doing a better job. They don't feel driven as they do in so many places outside of this country. They feel part of the team and they also have a future to look forward to.

So many members of American management have themselves been workers that their employees know that they, too, can, in many instances, look forward to promotion and more responsibility. The American system also challenges all segments of the economy to assume more responsibility, and by this alone prepares them to take on higher and better paying jobs. If their education has been too limited and they themselves cannot look forward to much advancement, they can always plan for their children by sending them to school and college and preparing them for a better life.

This is almost impossible abroad. Once a coal miner almost always a coal miner, and the children and grandchildren very often can look forward to being the same. This rigidity in the economic picture and this stratification of working classes, management classes, professional classes, etc., does not fire the population in foreign countries to the efforts that are needed to develop their economies. Such stratifications just don't exist in the United States.

These are some of the reasons why we in America do such a very large percentage of the world's business. We don't do so only because we have a larger country with fine natural resources, mineral and agricultural. Our greatest natural resource is our people, and it is the American people who have brought this country economically to the high state of development that we have reached in relation to the rest of the world.

These things are little understood abroad. They tend to see us as a people interested only in material things. Consequently, one of the most popular sports abroad is to discourse on American materialism. People all over the world like to dwell on the number of automobiles we have, the number of bathtubs, television sets, refrigerators, and our other material possessions. They have talked about how "money mad" we are for years.

We, unfortunately, have often aided and abetted this type of propaganda by our love of quoting statistics indicating how blessed we are with this world's goods. The exhibitions we have had abroad, at the Brussels Fair and in Moscow, have stressed our material possessions and left unemphasized other aspects of American life.

The picture painted in the minds of most foreigners is that the American is very rich, only concerned with his material welfare, and that he likes to boast about these things. Our tourists, who go abroad each year by the millions, have not always done very much to counteract this national image either. They are too often apt to be loud and boisterous, spending their money too ostentatiously.

This became so alarming to many thoughtful people

that it finally culminated in a letter which was sent to all recipients of American passports, signed by the President himself. This letter outlined how Americans should conduct themselves when they are traveling abroad. This is a most unprecedented document. Never in the history of the world has any head of any governmnent felt impelled to write a letter to every citizen who intends to travel abroad, telling him how to behave himself.

Our soldiers stationed abroad generally have a great deal more money to spend than is perhaps good for them. This means that they can compete on much more favorable terms for the local belles, a matter often resented by the men of the area. This natural resentment on their part is not to be wondered at when they see their girl friends being taken out by American G.I.'s who seem to be spending money literally like "drunken sailors." It only helps further to crystallize the image of American materialism.

Of course one reason the picture is so one-sided is that we have not tried hard enough to present the other side. No one has felt it important to present the American image in a more accurate light. No one has tried to publicize the fact that there are 109,000,000 church-goers in America, and that 63 per cent of the population belongs to religious institutions. Years ago, in 1835 to be exact, when the Frenchman, De Tocqueville, published his famous book after his trip around the United States, he wrote, "Not until I went into the churches of America and heard her pulpits flame with righteousness did I understand the secret of her genius and power."

When we compare this to the statistics available about

Europe we get quite a different picture. Only 10 per cent of the people in England attend church, 5 per cent of those in France, and 4 per cent of the people in some of the Scandinavian countries ever see the inside of a church. This indicates that a much larger percentage of Americans are interested in spiritual things than seems apparent to Europeans. It hardly goes with the popular European impression that we are rank materialists.

Also, there is no other country in the world where as much private money is donated to education as in the United States. New colleges and universities are constantly being founded, and large sums of money are donated each year to the established ones by private individuals. In Europe, on the other hand, it is very unusual to hear of the founding of a new university. Nor do you hear very often of private individuals giving large sums of money to educational institutions abroad. Much of this is left to the government to do. But our universities are constantly expanding and new ones are literally being founded every month.

Nor is there any other country in the world where such large sums are freely given to charity. I sat next to Nehru's sister one time at a large luncheon, the purpose of which was to raise money for the blind. She questioned me closely about it, and seemed amazed at the number of businessmen who were present. Finally she said, "You know, I can't imagine a businessman in India giving any money to an institution for the blind. It would be almost unthinkable."

I am afraid that we ourselves have given the world the impression that America's goal is materialism, inaccurate as that may be. It is true that materialism ranks very high in this country, too high perhaps, but not as high as is thought abroad.

Actually, there's nothing wrong with having the material things in life that make for well-being and leisure. It is what we do with those things that counts. The trouble is that many people are spoiled by prosperity. Adversity is often better for the moral character than good fortune. People generally work harder when they're having a tough time and slacken up considerably as soon as they make a little money. Those people, whose only goal is materialism, are apt to sit back and take it easy as soon as they have achieved it. This is one of the great dangers to our society. It makes us complacent, easy-going, and softens us up. Our real problem in America is learning how to live with prosperity.

The fact is that materialism is not America's primary goal. Materialism is just one of its by-products. It is one of the results of our way of life, rather than its aim.

Nor is freedom our primary goal, although I'm afraid we have misled the world into thinking that freedom is the sole aim of life in this twentieth century. Too much emphasis has been placed on freedom and freedom alone. But freedom alone is not enough. The important thing is what we do with it. And I think we are developing a more constructive attitude about it. I think we are gradually discovering that freedom is only the climate that God has given to the American people *within which* to work for, and finally to *achieve,* our real goal.

What, then, is the American goal? It certainly is

something that needs to be clarified so we can begin to comprehend it. I'm afraid we are almost as confused about it as is the rest of the world. I once tried to telescope a definition of the American goal into twenty-five words. My hope was that these twenty-five words could be memorized by school children and recited at proper times very much the way they now recite the Allegiance to the Flag. It seems to me necessary to start children thinking in the direction of a national goal so that finally the entire population of the United States will realize we really have one. We must demonstrate that we are not wallowing around in indecision. Our false goals must be placed in a proper perspective so that people will not be led astray.

Here is the definition I finally worked out. Although it is naturally very general in its wording, it seems to me to form a clear picture of America's goal:

The true goal of the American way of life is the creating of a self-reliant, individually responsible, self-disciplined, well-educated and spiritually oriented people.

Although this may seem to be getting quite far afield from the distribution revolution, actually it is not. There is nothing wrong in having material possessions provided they are seen in their proper perspective and provided our total values are right.

It is my firm belief that Providence wanted the human race to rise above poverty. I believe we are intended to manufacture and distribute enough of the world's goods so that men can be relieved of scrubbing and digging and so that eventually we can concentrate more and more on the spiritual and moral values of life. It is my firm belief that we are making steady, although sometimes halting, progress in this direction, and I feel that in the years to come it will be even more rapid.

During the past fifty years we in America have had to digest not only the physical immigration from Europe, but also the immigration of ideas that were based on concepts alien to our objectives. These ideas were remnants of problems that existed in Europe one hundred years ago and that have never really existed here.

We in America are not only blessed with a brandnew country, but by the fact that we started from scratch. We didn't have to undo the age-old barriers to progress that existed in Europe. We created, of course, some of our own problems, but by and large we were able to blaze new trails in almost every conceivable direction. Not only did our forefathers come here to blaze new spirituals trails, but new economic ones as well.

Certainly one of these new trails was our approach to distribution, which, coupled with American mass production, has brought this country economically to the highest point of development ever acheived in human history. This is nothing that we need to be ashamed of. When it is understood in its proper perspective, it will be realized that it is one of the great contributions that America has made to the world.

I cannot overemphasize the point that a clearer and more universal understanding of this is of primary importance. So much of the world is almost insanely trying to develop its production facilities, but owing to ignorance and misunderstanding is neglecting its distribution machinery. It is my hope that the world will discover this error soon. If it doesn't we are headed for an economic cataclysm that will make the depression of the 1930's seem mild. On the other hand, if the world does discover it in time, I think we can achieve the greatest era of economic development and the greatest era of true mass prosperity that have ever been conceived.